AMAZING SURVIVAL STORIES FOR ADVENTUROUS KIDS

16 TRUE STORIES ABOUT COURAGE, PERSISTENCE AND SURVIVAL TO INSPIRE YOUNG READERS

BILL O'NEILL

DON'T FORGET YOUR FREE BOOKS

CONTENTS

Introduction 1

Chapter 1: Your Plane Plummets into the Jungle 2

Chapter 2: Lost on A Maine Mountain 8

Chapter 3: My Family Shipwrecked by Killer Whales.............16

Chapter 4: Playing Hockey with Dad Helped Me Survive 23

Chapter 5: We Surfed a Mega-Tsunami and Lived 28

Chapter 6: Mom Raises Five Kids Alone in Wild Alaska 35

Chapter 7: Dogs Save Six-Year-Old from Freezing..................41

Chapter 8: Buried Alive by Avalanche, "Miracle" Boy
Emerges..49

Chapter 9: How Did Nine-Year-Old Mike Escape the
Peshtigo Fire? 53

Chapter 10: Look Out - Alligator Attack!...................................64

Chapter 11: Stuck in a Cave After Soccer Practice 69

Chapter 12: Barely Back from the Moon on Apollo 13..............79

Chapter 13: A Person Named Blackjack, Alone on An Island ..89

Chapter 14: Shackleton's Journey to The End of The Earth 97

Chapter 15: Will You Survive If You Run Away from Home?122

Chapter 16: Pasaban, The Queen of 8,000 Meters 127

Conclusion..137

INTRODUCTION

Kids like you and me love adventure. That's because we love to hear and learn about people, like us, who are adventurous in spirit, face and survive the most dangerous and difficult odds, and in the end find a way to make it through.

We need to warn you though! Not everyone included in these amazing stories lives to tell the tale. Family members and friends are lost forever. But all the heroes and heroines of our stories find a way to survive - whether it's because of their bravery, a fair dose of luck, using their wits - or all of the above.

Kids like us might not want to confront the natural disasters you'll find in this book, like avalanches and alligator attacks, or the harrowing situations in this book, like getting lost on a cold, foggy mountain, or inside a flooded cave for days on end. But we sure like to share these amazing and true survival stories - reading in the safety of our bedrooms, libraries, and schools!

CHAPTER 1:

YOUR PLANE PLUMMETS
INTO THE JUNGLE

This is the truly amazing story of teenager Juliane Koepcke. While flying over the Peruvian rainforest with her mother, their plane was struck by a bolt of lightning! The teen then survived a two-mile fall through thin air and found herself all alone - but still alive - in the dense jungle. She was just 17 years old at the time. Some 40 years later, she recalled what happened on that dreadful day.

These are her own words to describe an unbelievable adventure:

"It was Christmas Eve in 1971, and everyone was eager to get home. My mother was an ornithologist [somebody who studies birds], and my father was a biologist. We were also upset because the plane was seven hours late. Suddenly we entered into a very heavy, dark cloud. My mother was anxious, but I was fine at that point - I actually liked flying".

Yet only 10 minutes later, it was clear that something was very wrong. There was heavy turbulence, and the plane was literally jumping up and down, with parcels and luggage falling from the overhead bin. There were gifts, flowers, and Christmas cakes flying all around the cabin.

"When we saw lightning flashing around the plane, I got scared. My mother and I held hands tightly, but we were unable to speak. Other passengers began to cry and weep and scream.

After about 10 minutes, I saw an extremely bright light on the outer engine on the left. My mother spoke to me calmly - "this is the end - it's all over." Sadly, those were the last words I ever heard from her."

"The plane plummeted down in a terrifying nose-dive. It was pitch black, and people kept screaming. Then, all of a sudden, only the deep roaring of the engines completely filled my head."

"Suddenly, the noise stopped, and I was outside the plane. I was in a free-fall, strapped to my seat, but hanging upside down head-over-heels. The whispering and whooshing of the wind was the only noise I could hear. I felt totally alone."

"I could see the canopy of the jungle spinning towards me. Then I lost consciousness and remember nothing of the impact. Later I learned that the plane had broken into pieces about two miles above the ground. I woke up the next day and looked up into the canopy. The first thought I had was - 'I survived an air crash.' I shouted out for my mother, but I only heard the sounds of the jungle. I was completely alone."

"I had broken my collarbone, and had some deep cuts on my legs, but my injuries weren't serious. I realized later that I had ruptured a ligament in my knee, but I could walk. Before the crash, I had spent a year and a half with my parents at their research station only 30 miles away. I learned a lot about life in the rainforest - that it wasn't too dangerous. It's not the green hell that the world always thinks."

"I could hear the helicopters and planes overhead searching for the wreck, but it was a dense forest, and I couldn't see them. I was wearing a short, sleeveless mini-dress, and white sandals. I had lost one shoe, but I kept the other because I am very short-sighted and had lost my glasses. So, I used that shoe to test the ground ahead of me as I walked."

"Snakes are camouflaged there, and they often look like dry leaves. I was lucky I didn't meet them or maybe I just didn't see them. I found a small creek and walked in the water because I knew it was safer."

"At the crash site, I had found a bag of sweets. When I had finished them, I had nothing more to eat, and I was really afraid of starving. It was very hot and wet, and it rained several times a day. But it was cold at night, and to be alone in that mini dress was very difficult."

"On the fourth day, I heard the noise of a king vulture landing, which I recognized from my time at my parents' reserve. I was afraid because I knew they only land when there is a lot of carrion, and I knew they were after bodies from the crash."

"When I turned a corner in the creek, I found a bench with three passengers rammed headfirst into the earth. I was paralyzed by panic. It was the first time in my life I had seen a dead body."

"I thought my mother could be one of them, but when I touched the corpse with a stick, I saw that the woman's toenails were painted - my mother never polished her nails. I was immediately relieved but then felt ashamed of that thought."

"By the tenth day, I couldn't stand properly anymore, so I drifted along the edge of a larger river I had found. I felt so lonely, like I was in a parallel universe, far away from any other human being."

"I thought I was hallucinating when I saw a really large boat. When I went to touch it and realized it was real, it was like an adrenaline shot. But then I saw that there was a small path into the jungle where I found a hut with a palm leaf roof, an outboard motor, and a liter of gasoline."

"I looked at the wound I had on my upper right arm. It was infested with maggots about one centimeter long. I remembered our dog had the same infection, and my father had put kerosene on it. So, I sucked the gasoline out and put it into the wound."

"The pain was intense as the maggots tried to bury themselves further into the wound. I pulled out about 30 maggots and was very proud of myself. I decided to spend the night there. The next day, I heard the voices of several men outside. It was like hearing the voices of angels."

"When they saw me, they were alarmed and stopped talking. They thought I was a kind of water goddess - a figure from a local legend who is a hybrid of a water dolphin and a blonde, white-skinned woman.

"But I introduced myself in Spanish and explained what had happened. They treated my wounds and gave me something to eat, and the next day took me back to civilization.

"The day after my rescue, I saw my father. He could barely talk, and at first, we just held each other. For the next few days, he frantically searched for any news of my dear mother. On January 12, they found her body.

"Later, I found out that she also somehow had survived the crash but was badly injured and couldn't move. She died several days later. I dread to think what her last days were like. I also learned that I was the only survivor out of the 91 people on board that aircraft."

CHAPTER 2:

LOST ON A MAINE MOUNTAIN

Donn Fendler was totally lost on a cold, lonely mountain, just as the fog closed in. "I started to run, and found I couldn't, because of the boulders; that made me frantic, and I climbed over them like a cat and yelled and shouted and cried all the time. I yelled for my dad. I climbed up as high as I could on a big rock and screamed for him - then I waited. No answering shout - nothing - just the noise of the wind, and the purring sound of fine sleet driving against my clothes," he lamented.

Donn had gone ahead of his father on the trail, while hiking with an older guide's son, Henry. An elderly gentleman called to them, but Donn's teeth were already chattering from the plummeting temperatures. Henry spoke briefly to the older man, named Reverend Charles Austin, but Donn decided he'd go back to find his father. So, he left, alone. Suddenly, a heavy mist settled all around him, and his sight of the others vanished.

That was Donn's first and biggest mistake - to try to locate his dad by himself on a chameleon-like mountain in Maine where the weather conditions were rapidly getting worse - where fast-moving clouds, fog, and mist could quickly make even the strongest person's life miserable.

"I was nervous, too, and maybe that is why I decided to go right back and join Dad and the boys. Maybe I was sorry that I had gone on ahead of them. Maybe that had been a foolish thing to

9

do. Such thoughts run through a fellow's head at times like that. Anyway, they ran through mine and made me more and more anxious to get back to the folks below," Fendler recalled. If those were his thoughts at the start of his adventure, imagine how bad things got later on.

Nobody would see him again for nine days. The boy would drop from 74 pounds to 58, lose his pants, and toss his tennis shoes away because he was sure they'd shrunk. In fact, his feet were too inflamed to fit in them any longer. It's estimated that the youngster walked around 80 long miles during those nine days of walking barefoot while lost in the very wild Maine woods.

One guide specializing in the area, Earl W. York, Jr., later explained, "The stones are so sharp on parts of Mount Katahdin that a pair of new, heavy sneakers will not last over six trips - even when the regular trail is followed." Let's remember that this boy crisscrossed most of that area in his naked feet after leaving his "shrunken sneakers" behind.

When Reverend Austin met the boys at the beginning of this story, they were close to a dangerous spot called "The Knife Edge." That knife-like precipice has drop-offs in some places that plunge straight down 1,500 feet. Just picture Donn bumbling around in the dense fog, not even realizing how perilously close he came to such drop-offs! That drastic granite wall connects

Pamola (what the locals refer to as "the Demon Spirit") and Baxter Peak, the summit of Katahdin.

"Henry said I was foolish and tried to stop me, but I knew I was all right. I guess I thought I knew more than he did, for I only shrugged my shoulders and laughed at him. Just then, an extra heavy cloud rolled in around us. I thought of people being lost in clouds and getting off the trail - and maybe that hurried me a little as I pulled up my fleece-lined reefer about my neck and started down. Boy, I can see now what a mistake that was! A fellow is just plain dumb who laughs at people who know more than he does," remembered Fendler, with a chuckle.

In this most amazing story, and the ones to come, you'll meet lots of people who didn't know what they were doing, but a combination of common sense, grit, and good luck saw them through. Another thing we all need to understand is that in hiking, a "trail" doesn't always mean that it's a clearly marked one.

The Hunt Trail on Mt. Katahdin is only marked with spots of white paint on trees and rocks at some spots. Indeed, in this area, there are some arrows pointing toward Baxter Peak. But none of these marks would ever be seen in the white mist and hail - the same color as the silly painted spots!

Donn further elaborated on his dilemma - which way should he go to get home, or at least to meet somebody on that mean mountain who might help him find his desperate dad? "Everything looks different in the clouds. You think you see a man, and he turns out to be only a rock. It kind of scares a fellow, especially when you are alone and awfully cold," he said.

In the book he later wrote about his lengthy adventure, Donn recalls crawling through the so-called "pucker bush" which is a plant named Wax Myrtle. Most hikers avoid it at all costs. It's simply too thick and gnarly to walk through. In Felder's case, that pucker bush proved to be what saved him.

"Suddenly the pucker bush gave way under me, and I felt myself falling into a deep hole. I grabbed at the bushes as I went down and got hold of a big stem. For a moment I thought I was a goner! Boy, that hole was deep - twenty or thirty feet - and there were jagged rocks on the bottom. I just hung on to that pucker bush hoping that it would not tear out by the roots. I prayed a little too - just hung on and prayed," Donn admitted.

When you think about it, you realize it's much better to fall 20 feet than 1,500. After all the sleet and hail, Donn made his way out of the pucker brush and then saw a sign for Saddle Trail. However, he remembered hearing about it as a place "full of landslides and loose rocks." He worried that although it was finally a marked trail that would lead him somewhere, it might be "perhaps to some lonely spot miles and miles from camp."

At that point, almost freezing, famished for a bite to eat, and lonely beyond belief, he decided, "No, I mustn't take it." However, Saddle Trail, if he could have followed it safely, would have led him to a place named Chimney Pond, and then a bit further to Roy Dudley's camp, where there were people that very night. Of course, the young guy didn't know that, and survivors like Donn who look back on their amazing adventures don't have much use for hindsight.

During that first night on the mountain, there were 40-mile-per-hour winds. At times, even though it was the month of July, the temperature - together with the wind-chill factor - had dropped to 40 °F. Doctors and specialists wonder even now how he didn't get hypothermia (a condition that leads quickly to a person freezing, perhaps to death!). Especially with wet clothes and no shoes or pants.

Despite the horrible hunger he faced, along with bitterly cold temperatures at night, the ever-buzzing insects (the mosquitoes, leeches, blackflies, and moose flies that make Maine infamous, to name a few), along with black bears and other dangers during the day, young Donn never lost hope. He always imagined that right around the next corner, he would be rescued.

For those who make jokes about the insects, one seasoned guide, Harry Kearney, said, "The moose flies are by far the worst, but the bite of the copperhead - a tan, translucent fly, about half an inch long - can cause blood-poisoning unless cared for immediately." And you thought the bugs where you live were bad!

When asked if he was glad to see daylight come the next day, Donn quickly replied, "No!" Daylight only meant walking again on his swollen, throbbing feet, on top of his hunger, worry, and burning bug bites. Plus, he fretted that he was moving away from civilization, rather than toward it.

On July 27, 1939, the Boston Transcript reported: "But after the searchers had turned back, and after the press had pronounced this return hopeless, thousands of mothers in America did not give up hope. They scanned the papers daily for word; they watched their sons a bit more closely. There was a stout trail of hope being blazed for this boy."

The Maine State police force had two dogs called bloodhounds that were immediately rushed to a plateau. There, they picked up the unmistakable scent of the lost boy. The hounds led the search party to a place called Saddle Springs, where suddenly his trail was lost.

At that moment, the searchers themselves believed that Donn must have left the plateau and taken a deadly tumble somewhere between the big boulders surrounding the plateau. The two bloodhounds weren't used to that kind of unfriendly terrain. Their padded canine feet were quickly ripped and cut to such a degree that they had to be sent home for treatment.

Finally, Donn found a small creek, which he followed to a bigger stream. He followed that in turn and came to a camp where he met a man named Mr. McMoarn who knew all about the search going on for this ragged boy. The kind gentleman called the police, and Donn's mother and family were quickly notified.

Not satisfied to wait patiently at home, Donn's mother was taken by canoe toward that special cabin. In the meantime, an exhausted but relieved Donn was on his way downstream in another canoe. Can you picture the reunion the boy had with his mom when they finally met in mid-river? Although, they saved most of the hugs for later so as not to capsize the canoes!

CHAPTER 3:

MY FAMILY SHIPWRECKED BY KILLER WHALES

Imagine going for an afternoon sail with your family. Then your parents decide that they'd like to take you completely out of school so that you can go around the world on a boat (and you're still only nine years old). What's more - when you manage to get out in the middle of the world's biggest ocean, the one called the Pacific, a school of killer whales decides to hold you, hostage. So, school wasn't so bad after all, was it?

On top of that, you and your family have to survive in a dinghy (a ridiculously small boat) for more than a month with hardly any food or drinking water.

It sounds just like the most amazing fantasy story ever and surely must be taken straight from a classic adventure novel, right? Yet, this was the harshest of realities for the Robertson family from Staffordshire, England, while on an amazing journey around the globe during the 1970s.

When they were finally plucked from the open ocean by a Japanese fishing boat, some 40 years ago, their sensational story made every global headline.

It all began back in 1970, when a retired merchant navy officer named Dougal Robertson was running a dairy farm at Meerbrook, near Leek in the UK, with his wife Lyn, 18-year-old son Douglas, daughter Anne, then 17, and twin sons Neil and Sandy, both nine at the time.

"We lived in a very isolated situation," recalled Douglas, 58 years old and living in London at the time of this later interview. "My father thought that in order to offset that, he would take us around the world in a boat to educate his children in 'the university of life'." Most kids would probably prefer a slightly more normal university - on dry land, thank you very much.

On January 27, 1971, the family set sail from Falmouth in Cornwall on board a 43-foot wooden schooner called Lucette. They had purchased that magical seacraft with their life savings after selling the farm. "Father's planning for this journey was zero - we didn't even have a practice sail around the bay, before setting off around the world," quipped Douglas.

Just in case somebody asks you later, you might note that a basic plan usually helps a lot - especially when you dream of tripping around the globe on a relatively small boat!

"I always remember my dad at the wheel as we set sail from Falmouth, stamping on the floor and shouting 'Yee-Ha!' He was actually living his dream at that time. Then a wave broke across the bow, and the cold wet spray lashed our faces, and we suddenly got an inkling this wasn't going to be a walk in the park," Douglas remembered with a chuckle.

During the next year and a half, the family crossed the mighty Atlantic Ocean and stopped at various Caribbean ports.

However, after sailing for 17 months, they found themselves in the middle of the Pacific Ocean.

All of a sudden, the boat was surrounded by a pod of killer whales not far from the Galapagos Islands off the coast of Ecuador. In fact, they weren't just surrounded - they were hit by the black and white whales.

"The whole boat shook, and the keel must've cracked. There was a splintering noise of wood cracking; if you can imagine the sound of a tree trunk being snapped in two," explained Douglas. "I heard this splashing noise behind me, and there were three killer whales following the boat."

Even though wild (it's hard to imagine that some can actually be "tamed") killer whales are somehow NOT considered a normal threat to humans by specialists, Douglas - then just a teen - thought he would soon be "eaten alive."

The family members, along with Robin Williams, a student hitchhiker they'd picked up, scrambled onto an inflatable life raft and dinghy. Douglas recalled that "it was a 10-man raft, but it could only take five people comfortably.

We had bellows (a kind of air pump) to keep it inflated, but they broke after a few pumps, so I had to blow it up with my mouth. We were beset with problems from the moment we set sail on that raft." Dougal Robertson came up with the idea that they could maneuver the raft to the center of the Pacific, and then ride the counter-current back to the U.S.

The group only had a few cans of water and some rations on board, including dried bread, biscuits, onions, and fruit. They managed to survive on those for six full days. (There's nothing quite like munching on a raw onion to live another day, we might add.) After that, they were able to catch rainwater in containers, while they were kept busy hunting turtles and fish to keep themselves fed.

"Turtle was the mainstay of our diet. We drank its blood when we had no water, we dried its meat and rationed it, and stored it up," Douglas remarked. "We rendered the fat down in the sun to make oil which we rubbed on our skin and drank to keep us warm."

The inflatable raft became completely unusable after 16 days. Then, the six people crowded into the 10-foot-long dinghy, which they called the 'Ednamair'. They had to take turns sitting in the dry part of the small boat.

On July 23, 1972, after 38 days of making do on the Ednamair, they were finally spotted by a Japanese fishing trawler, the Toka Maru II, which recognized their distress flare.

"My dad had been sunk once before in Ceylon (now known as Sri Lanka) by the Japanese in 1942 (during World War II), and here they were in 1972 picking him out of the water and saving his life. He did say that if for no other reason than to be able to forgive the Japanese for what had happened, the trip was worth it."

Before he died from cancer in 1992, Dougal Robertson penned a book about the family's amazing adventure, which was called Survive the Savage Sea (he liked the letter "s", wouldn't you say?) and also ended up being a feature film.

He used the profits from the book to buy yet another boat and went to live in the more placid waters of the Mediterranean Sea, while his wife Lyn returned to farming.

Douglas decided to join the navy and ultimately became an accountant. After the family donated their dear 'Ednamair' to the National Maritime Museum in Falmouth, Cornwall, in 2008, Douglas authored his own book called The Last Voyage of the Lucette. Why did the world need one more book to capture the family's high-sea trials and tribulations? Well, Doug believed that the way his father told the story didn't give the other family members enough credit!

"I never regretted the trip, even in the darkest hours," stressed Douglas. "In a funny kind of way life had a quality to it, the quality of survival, the reward of seeing another sunset, another sunrise. We felt like wildlife must feel in the jungle: to live another day was our only goal."

After reading this, you know that you too, can go right out and pass that tough school test next week, get through that difficult interview you have coming up, or even enjoy your next trip to the dentist.

CHAPTER 4:

PLAYING HOCKEY WITH DAD HELPED ME SURVIVE

When Norman Ollestad first saw the photo of a nine-year-old Dutch lad named Ruben van Assouw, who was the only survivor of a horrible 2010 airplane crash in Libya that unfortunately took away the lives of his mother, father, and brother - along with 100 others - it felt strangely familiar to him.

Ollestad confirmed when seeing the two photographs, that these two boys (one of which was actually him) looked a lot alike since the former had also survived a plane crash as a youngster. In the separate photos, the pair both show the same ghostly black-and-blue eyes, although their expressions were surprisingly calm given that they'd just survived two life-shattering accidents.

"I was 11, when a Cessna carrying my father, his girlfriend, the pilot, and I crashed into an 8,600-foot peak during a blizzard. In the end, I was the only survivor, and had to make my way down a steep, icy mountain to safety, a nine-hour ordeal," Norman recalled.

Do you know what Ruben told the media after his crash? "I'm fine… I just want to go home," Ruben claimed. Norman admitted he had basically experienced the same feeling. "I couldn't wait to go home and play with the kids on my block. I just wanted things to be normal again - or as normal as possible. I didn't understand, or couldn't bear to understand, why people were taking my picture, and asking me so many questions, or why they cared so much," Ollestad remembered.

"'What else was I supposed to do?' I'd felt like asking the various reporters stuffing microphones in my face. 'Not trying to get down? And no, I don't know why I survived the impact of the crash, and my father did not.' I did know why I'd been able to navigate that merciless mountain. My father had spent years teaching me to stay calm under pressure - 'cool in the pocket' as they say in football and surfing - and I understood ice, snow, and mountainous terrain from skiing the backcountry with him. Ruben won't have any concrete explanation for his survival to lean on.

"I went right back to school and tried to wheedle my way back into my old life by playing with friends. I ignored or made light of inquiries about the crash. Each and every day, I spent most of my time and energy protecting myself from facing what I'd been through. I played it down in every way I could.

"But it started to wear me out. And this is something Ruben will have to deal with. He'll have to do something with the pain and the grief. Luckily, I got back into surfing, the sport my father taught me to love. That gave me a lot of joy and confidence and ultimately connected me back to my father, making his loss less bleak. Gradually, there evolved a silver lining - surfing, riding

25

waves, this skill he'd taught me, this gift, was keeping him alive in some way, allowing him to continue to be there for me.

"I was also lucky to have a godmother who supplied unconditional love and gave me license to grieve. I hope Ruben's aunt and uncle will play this role for him. Even though I kept my turmoil private and projected an air of 'I'm fine; what's the big deal?', I wasn't really fine. It was my godmother's quiet but steadfast acknowledgment of my pain that created a safe space for me to cope and remain stronger than the ever-looming, potentially crushing sorrow.

"I anticipate that Ruben will be encouraged to process the grief and pain with a therapist. In my time, it was not as embraced as it is today, and I believe I could have greatly benefited from psychotherapy. Not until I was 29 years old, did I finally seek counseling, and it really helped me heal because surfing could only take me so far.

"Ruben is special. Not even 10, he has endured two of the most monumental experiences a person can ever go through - the loss of a parent, and a close look at death -his own mortality. I hope he is given the time and guidance to navigate this road to healing. In the blink of an eye, he's been forced to grow up; as a young boy facing the journey of a far older man," Norman explained.

Norman's book, Crazy for the Storm: A Memoir of Survival, vividly tells his story of living through the 1979 plane crash in which his father perished. But the book is really much more than just a fiery plane crash.

It's more about his relationship with an adrenaline-crazed dad who soaked up the wildlife around Malibu in the 1970s and continuously pushed his own "Boy Wonder" to be the best, from the ski slopes of northern California to the crashing surf off the Mexican coast.

"It's actually 100 percent about my relationship with my father," Ollestad elaborated. "That relationship was present on the mountain with me, even though he was dead."

Norman is sure that what his father taught him (or forced him to do, depending on your viewpoint) saved his life. The skiing made him more aware of how steep the mountain's slope was, and what he had to do to get down it without falling. Skiing, surfing, and playing hockey with his dad gave him better control of his body, and the knowledge of the exact movements needed to work his way through the descent's riskiest spots.

"Some of it was sort of eerily, specifically perfect for the situation," he remembers. "A forty-five-degree pitch, a blizzard with ice - well, I've been here for eight years doing this. It was familiar to me."

CHAPTER 5:

WE SURFED A
MEGA-TSUNAMI AND LIVED

The name "mega-tsunami" is indeed not the title of a low-budget sci-fi movie. It's a very real, rare, and dangerous happening. It's much bigger and stronger than your average tsunami (a huge ocean wave that usually results from an earthquake). And it can form quickly, leaving you precious little time to escape.

On July 9, 1958, Howard Ulrich and his seven-year-old son were resting on their boat, enjoying a most pleasing day in Lituya Bay, Alaska. They woke up to a deep rumbling sound as their boat rocked violently. Soon they encountered several unpredictable waves created by a 7.8 magnitude earthquake. The earthquake was so strong enough that it could be felt as far away as Washington State.

To the horror of the father and son, they soon saw the mountains around them shake, rocks fall into the ocean, and a giant wall of water heading straight at them.

Luckily, their location at the far end of the bay allowed them a few minutes to escape. But the boat's anchor got stuck on the seabed! Ulrich tossed his son a life preserver and prepared for the end.

At 10:15 PM on July 9, 1958, the Great Alaska Earthquake badly shook a place called the Gilbert Inlet. The technical explanation was that the Fairweather Fault had slipped, setting off an earthquake that was measured between 7.8 to 8.3 on the Richter scale.

That triggered a chain of events that resulted in the largest mega-tsunami ever known in the history of humanity: the Lituya Bay Mega-Tsunami.

That earthquake was a kind called the "strike-slip" type. That's when two slabs of our planet move horizontally next to each other along a vertical fault line. When this nasty quake struck, it also released about 30 million cubic yards of rock from a cliff that went straight down into a narrow inlet (the one you heard about - Lituya Bay).

It wasn't a short distance into the bay either. All that rock and stuff fell from as high as 3,000 feet before it landed and moved an incredible quantity of water. That liquid was then pushed with great force through the narrow strip of water in the direction of the opening to Gilbert Inlet.

By the time it arrived at the passageway, the mega-tsunami's destruction totaled 1,720 feet in height. (Just to put that in perspective: this monster wave's height was much taller than the Empire State Building!) Over a thousand feet of ice was cut away from the Lituya Glacier.

Trees were ripped out by their roots like toys, the earth was washed away down to the bedrock, and anything and everything that stood in the way of the massive wave was demolished in the blink of an eye.

Running up to the boat's deck, Ulrich could see the monstrous wave forming. He recalled the experience in an article he wrote and published in 1960.

"The wave definitely started in Gilbert Inlet, just before the end of the quake," he explained. "It was not a wave at first. It was like an explosion or a glacier sluff. The wave came out of the lower part and looked like the smallest part of the whole thing. The wave did not go up 1,800 feet; the water splashed there."

In his article, Ulrich claimed that the wave hit his vessel only three minutes after he first spotted it. The 'Edrie' (the name of Ulrich's boat) was buoyed to the bay's southern shore and then sucked back into the roiling water near the center before Ulrich could get control again.

But that first wave wasn't the only bad one - he and his son were hit by numerous 20-foot-high waves that quickly followed. Somehow, they finally escaped the bay.

The wave's force neatly broke the vessel's anchor chain, which gave Ulrich the chance to maneuver. Then the wave carried the boat out to the middle of the bay.

Ulrich battled smaller waves that continued to pound his boat while trying to dodge uprooted trees and large chunks of ice racing by on the current. Ultimately, his son and the captain could leave the bay, miraculously without any harm. At the same time, five other people weren't quite so fortunate.

The Ulrichs had surfed and survived a colossal 1,719-foot-tall wave. The power of this specific mega-tsunami was so incredible that the damage was even tangible far from our Earth, in outer space (not that there's really anyone we know out there watching).

The water traveled high up to the forest line, tearing out trees and destroying every kind of vegetation. According to NASA, the tsunami wiped out approximately 988 acres of forest. The natural injuries to Lituya Bay are still in evidence to this very day.

Different from regular tsunamis that start in the middle of the ocean, beginning somewhat small before growing in size before they hit the land, mega-tsunamis are instantaneous.

They're a result of major impact events like meteor strikes and landslides (like you may have seen in the movies). The water travels straight out - a lot like when you see the ripples from a rock dropped into a pond.

Lituya Bay is a place where mega-tsunamis are very likely to happen (this may help you and your parents plan your next vacation!). The area also suffered from mega-tsunamis in 1854, 1899, 1936, and 1958. This is due to the place's location on the forever unstable Fairweather Fault, together with the always melting, uneasy ice of the local glaciers.

Now, so many years later, the proof of this enormous wave is still visible. A line of damage reaching up to 700 feet around the outside of the bay is visible when viewed from a plane or helicopter. It continues to be the spark of interest for many scientists.

It's interesting to think that this wasn't the first mega-tsunami to hit Lituya Bay.

There's plenty of evidence of at least five others over the past 150 years, with the first description coming from a certain Jean Francois de Galaup, the first European to make his way into the bay by sailboat.

In 1786, he wrote that all trees and vegetation had been ripped from the shoreline. Based on old photos taken between 1854 and 1916, there was at least one - more likely two - mega-tsunamis. In 1936, it's believed that another wave reached nearly 500 feet as it sprinted up the sides of the bay.

Since most kids who are 10 years old stand around four feet tall, you can just try to imagine body surfing this kind of "special wave." By the way, the biggest waves that professional surfers (and other crazies) encounter off the coast of Maui in Hawaii are 100 feet!

Will we witness another mega-tsunami in the future, you ask? People in the know think it's highly likely. Let's just hope we're at home safe on the sofa when we see it - and not in the middle of that deceiving bay, taking a nice nap on our boat.

CHAPTER 6:

MOM RAISES FIVE KIDS ALONE IN WILD ALASKA

In the 1970s, lots of Americans were witnessing the birth of the home computer, plus the first video games, and the special magic of the microwave oven. Meanwhile, Norma Cobb and her family turned to a faraway, very wild place called Alaska where most of these gadgets didn't mean much of anything.

Cobb, along with her husband Lester and their five children, decided to head north to Alaska where they would follow their dream of claiming land under the Homestead Act. These were several laws that let people take ownership of government or public domain land to encourage settlement. The Cobbs were members of the last group of people to do so in the 49th state (the U.S. has 50 states, in case you're interested, with Hawaii rounding out that grand number).

The only land available at the time was in a place called the Minook Valley, north of Fairbanks, and near the cold, dark Arctic Circle. But the Cobbs were undaunted, so they forged on, living in Fairbanks during the winter for their first two years, and then in a tent on the 80 acres they were given by the government during the summer as they slowly built their cabin.

"Our first cabin had vertical logs because I wasn't strong enough to help Lester lift them. The kids helped chink the spaces with tundra," Cobb recalled while kicking back in her current home in the Village of Oak Creek. "It fell down with the first snow, but we just rebuilt it again."

When Cobb first moved to Alaska, she was a young mom at 27 years old, with her husband Lester, only 21. The children stretched in age from Norma Cobb's nine-year-old daughter to a one-year-old baby. Lester looked for work that often took him far from home. At one point, both Lester and Norma labored on the Trans-Alaskan Pipeline. Lester drove a truck, while Norma busied herself in the kitchen.

"The men didn't like me there much," she said with a smile. "The first five years were the toughest. That's when we learned everything. We were tenderfeet." According to the Homestead Act, an individual must "prove up" on the property. That meant they had to make improvements to the land within the first five years before they could register for a document to own it. Usually, a house was considered enough, according to the act.

The majority of families hopped in their cars and went to the grocery to buy food. But it was a bit more difficult for the Cobbs. The nearest town for them was almost 20 miles away. They also shopped in Fairbanks, some 150 miles to the south, about twice a year. In the meantime, they hunted moose and bear, wild animals that were plentiful in the woods where their land was located.

"We never went anywhere, even to the outhouse, alone or without a gun. Up there, bears rule," Cobb laughed. Everyone, including the kids, helped with everything. When they hunted, the family cut up the meat for food, taking other parts of the animals to create items such as hats and gloves. The teeth and claws were made into rugged jewelry, which they then sold. To this day, Cobb wears a special necklace sporting a still-sharp bear claw.

"Up there, nothing went to waste," she claimed. After the Cobbs met the Homestead Act requirements, they got into gold mining and did pretty well, finding a few sizeable nuggets, including some that were a half ounce or more. A few years after, they completed a larger cabin on the other side of the creek.

To stay clean, they set up an outdoor shower, running water from the creek into a 55-gallon container suspended over a fire, and then piping the water downhill to a shower stall. They could only use the makeshift shower in the summer though.

During the long winter, the family got around by dog sled, boasting a team of Siberian huskies. At night, they read as much as possible and played lots of games. Cobb served as a teacher for her children in correspondence school. They also read the Bible and discussed the chapters, although there wasn't a single church anywhere nearby.

All the kids were raised on the homestead. One son continues to live in the wilds of Alaska while working on an oil pipeline, according to the mom. "For 20 years, I had no conveniences, except propane lights and a stove. Toward the end of our time up there, we got electricity and a telephone. It was like Christmas," she chuckled at the memory.

Cobb exited Alaska some years ago, after 31 full years of toughing it out in the wilderness. She and Lester divorced, and she decided she didn't want to go it alone in the wild. They sold some of their land and divided up the rest. At first, Cobb moved closer to her family in Nebraska where she grew up but said the weather was unsuitable. She'd traveled through Sedona, Arizona, as well as the laid-back community called the Village of Oak Creek, so, she decided to give it a go there.

"I miss the Northern Lights, and my cold, cold, clean water out of the creek, and the great mountain views we had in all directions. I visit every year with the kids though. Alaska was a paradise, and a land of extremes," she mused. "Summers were hot - up to 90 degrees and the coldest it ever got was 80 below (zero). The most snow we saw up there was 18 feet." You can definitely make a few snowballs out of that!

Even though homesteading in Alaska is well behind her now, Cobb admitted that she has no regrets. "I'd do it all over again.

So would my kids. They missed having friends, but realize they've had the opportunity to do things most people will never have," Cobb explained. "A lot of people dream of a life like we had."

Cobb wrote a book about her family's many adventures called Arctic Homestead. It was published in February 2003.

CHAPTER 7:

DOGS SAVE SIX-YEAR-OLD FROM FREEZING

If you have a dog, try your best to treat it very well - who knows - it may just save your life! After more than four hours, from the time his panicked parents announced that their six-year-old boy was missing from his southwest Missouri home, rescuers finally found the chilled child hunkered down in a ditch. His two dogs were lying on top of him, keeping him toasty. Temperatures outside had dropped into the low 20s (in Fahrenheit degrees, that is).

Little Ryle Smith was just having some fun outside his Seneca home on a normal Friday afternoon when he accompanied his dogs, Baxter and Bella, into the nearby woods. But he soon got mixed up and ended up lost as darkness descended around him. After looking high and low for his son, dad Ryan Smith phoned the authorities asking for help around 6:00 pm, the Joplin Globe reported.

"I was nervous because it was getting dark, and some of the area in the woods can be really dangerous," the concerned father said. "He was outside with the dogs, and we didn't see or hear from either of them." Emergency helpers from the Joplin, Seneca, and Redings Mill fire departments, as well as the Newton County Sheriff's Office and Newton County Rescue and Recovery team, all jumped into the rescue efforts.

"We got into action quickly, and that's what helped us find him," Sheriff Ken Copeland claimed. "The Highway Patrol chopper was even in the area with infrared to see if they could help. It really was an area-wide search that got him home."

Smith reported that his son was ultimately checked at a Joplin hospital and was basically unhurt, even though he was found without any shoes, a few cuts and scratches on his body, and several holes in his clothes. The dad gave tons of credit to the loyal dogs - Baxter, a big Boxer who's been part of the family for more than a decade, and Bella, a mixed Labrador, who joined the family at Christmas. They did a great job keeping Ryle safe and, most importantly, warm.

"They both were incredible in the way that they protected him," Smith gushed. "They wouldn't have left him for anything. You can't ask for more in a dog than that." The dad also acknowledged his extreme gratitude to the numerous people in the area who leapt into action.

"It amazes me how quick everyone came out to look for my son," he exclaimed. "An hour after word got out, you couldn't get anywhere close to the driveway. I still haven't got to meet the men who actually found Ryle, but I just want them to know how thankful we are."

Maybe you've heard the saying that dogs are man's (that's actually a little restrictive - let's say people's) "best friends." We could go on and on about the loyalty of our canine friends. But let's start with a few other short stories to make us all feel good and glowing at night. (The only question we really can't answer right now is: Why can't people be as nice to other people as dogs can?!)

Austin Forman, an 11-year-old boy, was also messing around in his yard when a cougar suddenly charged him from out of nowhere. Before he could do anything, his dog sprang in front of him to ward off the wild animal. The 18-month-old Golden Retriever courageously fought off the much bigger cougar so that the boy could escape to safety. The family quickly called 911, and a local policeman decided that the cougar had to be put down.

The brave dog, aptly named Angel, was seriously hurt after her fight with the cougar, but she came back to make a complete recovery. She now spends her days with her appreciative human family and the kid who knows he has a guardian angel in the furry form of a dog.

Another tall tale involved Jason Breiding who sadly watched his home burning to the ground. When he quickly accounted for his family, he realized in one heart-stopping moment that one of his kids wasn't present. As quickly as he perceived the danger, the family dog came racing out of the flames gingerly carrying the infant by its diaper!

The Breidings lost most of their possessions in the fire that day. Yet as Jason rocked his infant daughter, he realized that they still had everything that really mattered - thanks to the family's heroic puppy. The dog, a mixed breed, was amazingly not hurt by the fire.

Then there was Debbie Parkhurst, who didn't know what to do when she began choking on an apple. Before she could figure out how to help herself, her dog, Toby, jumped onto her chest and managed to dislodge the apple. The American Society for the Prevention of Cruelty to Animals (ASPCA) was so thrilled by the Golden Retriever's efforts that they gave him a fancy award.

And what happened to Stacie Pitts? At the beginning of this amazing adventure, Stacie was simply annoyed when Miley, the family dog, kept waking her up. She tried to get back to sleep and hoped Miley would calm down. However, Miley was persistent and kept waking her, until Stacie realized that something was very wrong.

Stacie quickly woke up her entire family, and they all found that each felt strangely sick, suffering from nausea and awful headaches. After going to the hospital, the family discovered that their pooch Miley had miraculously woken them, saving their lives from carbon monoxide poisoning.

By the way, the smell of carbon monoxide is that not-so-strong but sickening one that you experience when you stand next to a car that's running - especially in a closed space like a garage. Beware, and get some fresh air!

You'd also probably never guess that your average dog can handle a phone call. We know that young kids nowadays are better with tech gadgets than their parents, but dogs? Well, when Kevin Weaver collapsed from a diabetic-induced seizure, his dog Belle knew exactly what to do. The 17-pound Beagle bit into her master's phone to ring 911!

If Belle hadn't called for help, Weaver would have died. Belle is really a so-called therapy dog who's specially trained to detect Weaver's blood sugar levels. She often licks his nose to check his sugar levels and is trained to call 911 by biting at the numbers on the phone, if help is needed. When Belle senses that his sugar levels are out of whack, she whines and paws at him to remind him to check his blood sugar level.

And have you ever heard of a baby playing with a rattle toy? Yes, it's quite common. And how about a rattlesnake "playing" with a baby? In this particular case, it wasn't all fun and games for the tot. Booker West, a 12-month-old kid, was innocently splashing water in his backyard bird bath when a rattlesnake quickly cornered him and tried to strike.

Within moments, a five-pound Chihuahua named Zoey charged into high gear, rushed the snake, and attacked it. When the snake couldn't get to the kid, it bit the dog. But, at the end of the day, little Zoey made a complete comeback. Her act of pure bravery saved the baby from a poisonous snake bite. Canine courage comes in all shapes and sizes.

Now you need to know about Norman, a Labrador Retriever who's blind. Even so, he loved to get out and run on the beach with his owner, Annette. He adored the freedom of the beach because it was the only public place where he could safely run free. Thus, he didn't think twice when he heard a girl crying for help in the water. Despite his blindness, Norman dove straight into the drink to save the little girl who was drowning.

Guided by her constant shrieks, Norman eventually found her and gently led her to shore. She was clearly shaken, but in one piece, and still breathing. The brave dog didn't let his lack of sight stop him from saving a child in dire distress.

You may have already guessed it, but for centuries, people and dogs have shared a very deep bond. Recent research on this type of bond shows that there's a hormonal response in both dogs and their human owners that resembles the bond that exists between parents and their kids.

Dogs of every breed and size are quick to defend and help the people in their pack. Some dogs, like Norman the blind Labrador Retriever you just heard about, even show an abundant sense of nobility and courage while helping any human in need. These amazing stories of dogs aiding humans in their pursuit to survive reveal the loving, brave spirit of dogs, and the loyalty they give to those they love.

CHAPTER 8:

BURIED ALIVE BY AVALANCHE, "MIRACLE" BOY EMERGES

When you see avalanches cascading tons of snow down mountains on TV, you normally don't see any people. But a 12-year-old boy survived for 40 lengthy minutes after being buried under an avalanche in the French Alps. According to his rescuers, that was an achievement they could only term "a miracle."

The boy happened to be skiing on an off-piste part of the slopes at the La Plagne ski resort in Mâcot-la-Plagne. Suddenly, he was swept away and separated from his group, the French police told The Associated Press. Officials reported that he was moving down the slope ahead of seven other skiers, and out of nowhere was "caught when a large section of snow detached and roared down the mountain."

The deluge of snow, ice, and some good-sized rocks carried the boy at least 110 yards, but it was unclear how deeply he was buried under the White fluffy stuff. The region of the Alps where the avalanche happened had received a huge amount of snowfall earlier the same month, after a late start to the ski season. Many local resorts stayed shut longer than expected.

The boy wasn't wearing a jacket fitted with an avalanche detector, but he was still eventually found by a rescue dog, the kind that's trained to detect the vague scent of a human buried deep under the snow, at an altitude of 7,875 feet.

What are the odds of surviving for 40 minutes in such adverse conditions? Extremely low! National Geographic informs us: "Statistics show that 93 percent of avalanche victims survive if dug out within 15 minutes. Then the survival rates drop fast. After 45 minutes, only 20 to 30 percent of victims are alive. After two hours, very few people survive."

Pistehors.com reports that during the time between 15 and 45 minutes, almost two-thirds of victims die of asphyxiation, which means they take their last breath. "During this period, the surrounding air will either be exhausted, or the victim's respiration will condense and freeze slowly, rendering the surrounding snow impermeable." If you were paying attention in your chemistry class, that basically means that nothing can get in or out - including precious air and water.

"We can call it a miracle," Captain Patrice Ribes exclaimed, according to The Associated Press. "A day after Christmas, there was another gift in store." The boy did suffer a broken leg and was carried to Grenoble hospital, where he was placed under close observation, Euronews told the world.

"He was dragged several hundred meters without being crushed by the force of the snow," the commander of the Savoie Mountain Police, Patrice Ribes, reported. Amazingly, after this snowy roller-coaster ride, the boy "did not inhale any snow."

Ribes called for caution in the face of uneven snow cover conditions anywhere above 2,500 meters (8,202 feet). The young skier was able to avoid suffering from asphyxiation due to the "poor quality" of the snow, which allowed for good air circulation, according to the emergency services.

A team of piste workers from La Plagne had just been dropped off by helicopter on a slope opposite the avalanche. They saw it go off and so could effectively limit the search area.

About 30 people, including members of the ski patrol and ski-lift workers, were quickly mobilized to start probing the snow and were soon joined by gendarmes (the French name for armed police officers) from the Courchevel mountain rescue team.

"He was conscious when he was found because he shouted when he heard the sound played out by the gendarme," Luc Nicolino, piste manager, exclaimed. "He had a small amount of snow in his mouth, and knee and thigh pain, but the doctor wasn't worried about him," he added.

French Interior Minister Christophe Castaner jumped on Twitter to congratulate Gétro, the rescue dog, and his handler, Raphaël Chauvin, who worked together to locate the child under that heavy mass of snow. Playing and skiing in the snow can sure be a blast - until you're caught in an avalanche!

CHAPTER 9:

HOW DID NINE-YEAR-OLD MIKE ESCAPE THE PESHTIGO FIRE?

What would you think and do if you came face to face with the deadliest fire in American history? That's exactly what happened to eight-year-old John Kramer on that fiery night of October 8, 1871, in a place called Peshtigo, Wisconsin.

Have you ever heard of "The Great Chicago Fire" which scorched that big city way back in 1871? That terrible blaze occurred on the same night as Peshtigo, and while it was surely awful, it wasn't quite as bad as the inferno that John and his family faced. But the dry weather conditions and prevailing winds were very similar, leading to two huge, deadly fires in different states—on the very same night.

It had certainly been a difficult but action-packed year for John and his family, including his parents, Joseph and Katherine, and his nine-year-old brother Mike. The Kramers had managed to immigrate to the U.S. from Germany in the 1860s, settling first in the rolling farmland of upstate New York. Then, in 1870, they headed west to the relatively young state known as Wisconsin, full of that aggressive animal called the badger, and lots of opportunities for hard-working folks.

Thousands of new immigrants had made that same westward journey in the 1860s, attracted by the promise of inexpensive farmland, and the opportunity to carve a brand-new life out of the pristine, undeveloped American backcountry. And what a wilderness it was!

In the 1860s, an enormous forest stretched across Wisconsin and neighboring states like Minnesota. There were literally billions and billions of green trees, covering thousands of square miles of rich land. These were truly the forests of fairy tales, packed with towering trees and thousands of sparkling lakes, along with packs of howling wolves and bears who had pointed claws just like deadly daggers.

The writer known for the Little House series, Laura Ingalls Wilder, was also born in a cabin in the northern woods of Wisconsin only three years before the Kramers had settled in the same area. Describing the land where her family had found their own piece of paradise, she penned, "The great, dark trees of the Big Woods stood all around the house, and beyond them were more trees. As far as a man could go to the north in a day, or a week, or a whole month, there was nothing but woods."

Laura wasn't stretching the truth. The massive forest that stretched across northern Wisconsin was truly exceptional. For centuries, those woods were mostly undisturbed by humans. The only sounds were those of nature - the pleasant chirps of birds, the low growls of wild animals, and the hushed whisper of tree leaves rustling in the fresh breeze.

By the time John and his family made their way to Wisconsin, huge changes were happening in those woods. In the late 19th century, American cities were growing dramatically - especially a big midwestern one called Chicago, only 250 miles south of Peshtigo. Just 40 years before, Chicago was considered a small town on a marsh full of pesky mosquitoes!

But by 1871, it was the fastest-growing city in the whole wide world. It seemed that new buildings sprang up every day, including department stores and shops, factories, warehouses, and magnificent mansions. To fuel all this quick construction, the builders of mighty Chicago needed wood and more wood - at a constant rate. They didn't need to go that far to find it in the sprawling forests of Wisconsin.

In the 1860s, timber companies began to buy up big chunks of the northern woods. Then they dispatched armies of lumberjacks to hack down the trees, which they proceeded to strip off all their branches, dragged by oxcart and horse-drawn wagons across the forest floor, and deposited them in the roiling waters of the Peshtigo River. This river's rushing currents carried the giant logs downstream to the sawmill in the town of Peshtigo. It hummed all day long, cutting and transforming the trunks into lumber suitable for building.

By 1870, the forests surrounding Peshtigo boomed with the shouts and swear words of muscular lumberjacks, along with the never-ending chopping sounds of innumerable axes, and the thunderous noise of 150-foot-tall trees crashing to the ground all around. After a forested area had been cleared of trees, the lumber barons were glad to sell the land to farmers and settlers like John's parents.

Right away, the Kramers felt at ease in Wisconsin since there were numerous fellow immigrants from Germany and other parts of Europe. A little more than a year after their arrival, they'd already finished building their new house. The boys were growing as fast as the forests were coming down. Then came the day of the unforgettable fire.

Soon after moving to Wisconsin, the Kramers discovered that fires were a fact of life in those northern woods. Some fires were undoubtedly started by lightning. But the majority were started intentionally by people. The lumberjacks lit fires to get rid of the branches they'd chopped off the trees. Farmers used fire to try to clear their land of unsightly tree stumps and brush that the lumberjacks had left in their wake.

Sometimes, there were so many fires blazing and sizzling at the same time that a choking fog drifted ominously over the town of Peshtigo. The early part of 1871 was particularly a nasty time for fires. Precious little rain had fallen that summer, and the entire midwestern region was parched. Creeks and streams had dried up, and trees had withered without water.

On September 24, a series of fires began to burn out of control in and around Peshtigo. The blazes soon scorched hundreds of acres of forestland while incinerating homes and shops in nearby communities. When Peshtigo's largest factory caught on fire, hundreds of men rushed in to fight the leaping flames with buckets of water they drew as fast as possible from the river.

They managed to save the building, but dozens were badly hurt in that physically draining fight. The deadly fire proceeded to cast a spell of fear over the entire town of Peshtigo. A few people were so shaken that they quickly packed and left the village for good. But most families lacked the money to start life again somewhere new. All they could do was try to prepare better for the next inferno.

One Catholic priest in the town, Father Peter Pernin, decided to bury the precious bowls and goblets that belonged to the church under the ground. Farmers made it a point to leave wet blankets in their barns to protect their animals from airborne sparks. The Kramers carefully cleared their land of every last piece of dried brush and wood. Yet, in the end, there was simply no way to get ready for the terror soon to come.

October 8 arrived, and the day started strangely hot. The sky glowed an eerie orange color from the many small fires still smoldering in the forest. Suddenly, John's parents could see flames licking at the edge of the forest that surrounded their house. They quickly sensed that disaster was close at hand. While they were set on saving their beloved house, they also wanted their two sons well out of the fire's fatal reach.

Their neighbor's farm had a sizeable 40-acre field that was freshly plowed and free of trees and brush that could possibly burst into flames. Mrs. Kramer told her boys sternly to stay put in the middle of the empty field, waiting there until either she or their father would come to rescue them. Doom surely filled John's racing heart as he and his brother Mike timidly headed to the open field. Would they ever see their dear parents again?

As the day wore on, the smoke grew thicker, and the sky turned the rich red color of blood. Strong winds whipped through the area. Many prayed that somehow a soaking rain would arrive, and the peril of fire might pass. But there'd be no rain at all that night. Only violent, swirling gusts of wind that fanned the small fires in the forest persisted.

Those fires in turn just grew bigger and more dangerous until they ultimately joined into one colossal hellfire. Flames soared hundreds of feet into the darkening sky. Trees exploded into millions of sparks in the extreme heat. Flaming hunks of wood flew across the forest, carrying fire to places many miles away.

At 10:00 pm., the residents of Peshtigo were shocked to hear an ear-splitting roar that Father Pernin later described as something similar to the sound of an onrushing freight train. In fact, it was the noise generated by the uncontrollable fire itself - a blaze of inexplicable heat, power, and size - which erupted out of the forest.

The fire had become a firestorm. Indeed, it was a rare kind of inferno that happens when high winds meet great amounts of burnable material, like trees, that feed the hungry flames. Firestorms burn way hotter than normal wildfires, creating their own swirling wind and deadly explosive gases. Sadly, for most of the people close by, that haunting sound of the fire blasting from the forest was the final noise they would ever hear again.

In the meantime, John's parents escaped their house mere moments before the gigantic explosion. They knew their house wouldn't last. Now their only wish was to be reunited with their precious boys. They fled their home with a single possession: a mattress stuffed with feathers. The parents struggled with it towards the plowed field.

But they soon saw that there was absolutely no way to reach the field. Flames danced all around them, encircling the Kramers from every direction. It seemed like the air itself was on fire. All appeared hopeless for the couple until they came upon a drinking well. They forced their mattress into the water, soaking it through and through. They then quickly climbed inside the well and laid the wet mattress on top of themselves.

The Kramers cowered inside the well, clutching each other in total terror. They couldn't even begin to imagine the abject scenes of anguish that went on that night in their town of Peshtigo. The wall of heat and mammoth flames took the lives of hundreds of people in an instant.

Many others perished while trying to reach the safety they thought the river offered. The Kramers could hear the fire booming above them. They said their last prayers, never expecting to live out the night. Meanwhile, John and Mike didn't know what to think or do as they continued to squat together in the middle of the neighbor's plowed field.

The fire raged on for hours on end, wiping out Peshtigo and 16 more towns further to the north. By the next morning, more than a billion trees had been completely burned. A space twice the size of Rhode Island (all right - we know it's not that big of a state) was little more than an ocean of roasted tree trunks amidst grey and black ash, as far as the eye could see.

Nobody knows how many people really died, though many say that it was probably between 1,000 and 2,500. But miraculously, the whole Kramer family lived through the blaze to see the dawn of another day. After the flames died down the next morning, John and Mike staggered out of the field in search of their parents.

Joseph and Katherine eventually climbed out of the well from under their moist mattress, shivering despite the heat of the fire above, and went to find their long-lost sons. John admitted many years later that the sheer joy of finding each other alive again saw them through the extremely hard months that were to follow. Peshtigo and the surrounding areas had to cope with the terrible toll of death and destruction.

Their house and town were momentarily wiped off the face of the earth, along with many of their friends and neighbors. But they decided to stay on in Wisconsin to help the region and state rebuild and regroup. At the age of 81 when he finally passed away, John was still living there. He was surrounded by his six children and four grandkids when he finally went to a better place.

History books don't say a whole lot about the Great Peshtigo Fire. Yet John's children and grandchildren will go to their graves knowing that their fortunate grandfather amazingly lived through the deadliest fire that the American nation ever experienced.

And just in case you haven't heard enough about killer fires yet, as we mentioned, the Great Chicago Fire happened on the very same night as Peshtigo (due to similar weather conditions). After all was said and done, about 3.5 square miles of Chicago lay in ruin, with 18,000 buildings burned to the ground, and 300 people had lost their lives.

News of the Chicago fire spread quickly, and aid poured in from nearby states. Even the Wisconsin governor himself, Lucius Fairchild, rushed to Chicago to help with relief efforts. At the same time, Peshtigo's telegraph system and railroads had all been wiped out, which cut the poor city off from the outside world.

Those who survived (many with indescribable fire-related injuries) suffered for days in weather that suddenly turned cold. Their desolation continued for days until news of the disaster finally got through to government officials in Madison, the capital city of Wisconsin. As the governor was away, his wife Frances did her best to organize the rescue efforts.

You may read today that the Great Chicago Fire was a monumental event in U.S. history, while the Great Peshtigo Fire seems to have been almost forgotten.

CHAPTER 10:

LOOK OUT - ALLIGATOR ATTACK!

Alligators sure seem to have a lot of teeth. A 10-year-old kid from Florida found that out the hard way in 2017 while sitting on the sunny shore of a lake in Orange County on a seemingly normal day. Juliana's relaxing afternoon suddenly came to a screeching halt when an 8.8-foot-long alligator chomped into her knee and calf muscle. Ouch!

At first, the girl reacted by punching the prehistoric predator in the face, but her attempt to loosen its grip didn't have any effect on the Jurassic lizard. Then, she remembered a lifesaving fact she's learned at 'Gatorland', an alligator amusement park (we're not quite sure how much entertainment your average alligator can give you, but...). Jamming her fingers into the animal's nose, the girl waited and hoped it wouldn't be able to breath. Soon enough, miraculously, she was able to pry its mouth open.

After the gator let her loose, the girl jumped up screaming and shouting, and managed to run away. Her family took her to the hospital, where she received numerous stitches for her deep puncture wounds. Other than that, she was practically fine. Authorities dealt with the attack by catching the offending alligator and closing the lake for public swimming for some time to prevent similar accidents. Luckily, Juliana's quick thinking came to her rescue that particular day, and nobody else was injured.

While we're chatting about gators, you might as well know about the amazing adventure of six-year-old Joey Welch and his dad, Joseph, who were planning a spin in a canoe around the Loxahatchee Wildlife Refuge in Boynton Beach, Florida. While preparing to head out, Joey fell off the pier and landed in shallow water.

Before Joseph realized what had happened, he heard a scream and saw that an alligator had his son's arm in its massive jaws! The gator tried to drag the boy deeper into the water. Joseph didn't hesitate to jump in after his son. He punched the alligator repeatedly in the head, but it still wouldn't release the boy.

"He could have squished my son's arm like a cracker!" Joseph exclaimed later. Luckily, all the commotion got the attention of an onlooker who risked his own life by jumping into the water and going at the beast, kicking its underbelly several times. Under this constant beating, the alligator gave up and released little Joey.

Miraculously, the boy, who was taken to a nearby hospital, escaped with just a few scrapes and cuts - all thanks to the unknown rescuer, Joseph recalled. Since the father and son were in such a rush to get to the hospital, they didn't even get a chance to get to know their savior. "We don't know who this good

Samaritan was, but he's a big hero. Stepping in to help save someone else's child takes courage and compassion."

Then, in 2011, David Bostwick and his seven-year-old son were swimming at Wekiwa Springs State Park in Orlando, Florida, when an alligator came out of nowhere and took a bite of Bostwick. "I felt a gator's mouth clamping down on my head," he recalled. The dad reached up with his free arms, grabbed hold of the alligator's jaws and pried them open with all of his might.

The animal ultimately let him go, and Bostwick was taken to the hospital where his injuries were treated with 50 stitches, along with a few well-placed staples. "It's the kind of thing you think can never happen to you," he remarked.

And what about this? Back in 1992, Craig DeArmond of French Settlement, Louisiana, found a 10-foot alligator itching for a fight directly under his home! For half an hour, DeArmond, then 32 years old, battled the outsized reptile until he managed to wriggle himself free from the muck surrounding his home.

But just as he was busy clawing his way out of the muddy depths of his property, the alligator lunged, grabbing his leg, and pulling him back down, dragging him in the direction of the river. Yet DeArmond wasn't quite ready to give up.

He did everything he could to escape the toothy animal and eventually freed himself from its vice grip. DeArmond staggered over to his neighbor's house, and then was escorted to the hospital, where he received around 200 stitches to treat all the gator bites.

CHAPTER 11:

STUCK IN A CAVE AFTER SOCCER PRACTICE

Most of us head straight for the hot shower, and then home for a tasty meal, after soccer practice. However, in June of 2018, just after their training session, 12 members of a Thai youth soccer team called the Wild Boars and their coach decided to try something new: explore the nearby Tham Luang cave, one of Thailand's longest. They were intending to stay for about an hour.

The boys, ages 11 through 16, and their 25-year-old coach, Ekkapol Chantawong, waded into the shallow waters to start their cave exploration. Out of nowhere, a flash flood caused by the monsoon rains hit, and the group was pushed deeper inside the dark tunnel. They eventually found their way to relative safety an elevated platform almost four kilometers into the cave system.

The team would remain stuck underground for more than two weeks in what was to become a global media sensation. Since the adventure in the large Tham Luang cave network was supposed to be a quick one, the team had brought only a rope, a flashlight, and a few batteries - but they didn't have any extra water or food.

"When we went in, we got stuck in the cave. At that moment, we saw water. It was full of water," the coach later informed ABC News. "I then volunteered to dive to find out if I could go through or not. If I could go through, then everybody is saved. So, we used the rope that we brought with us."

But he was unable to escape, so the boys hauled their coach back in, and the days dragged on before they were at last discovered and reached by rescuers. Starving for any kind of food, and also quickly running out of precious oxygen, the team survived by drinking fresh water that dripped from a cave stalactite, while repeating their special mantra "su us" - in Thai, which means "keep fighting." They repeated it again and again to try to remain calm.

The flood filled the twisted cave system with water, trapping the boys for no fewer than 17 days. For the first nine of those days, they managed with no food, and could only rely on those dripping stalactites for water. But in fact, they didn't just sit around and wait for a miracle to happen.

Realizing they were trapped, the boys took turns digging a 16-foot hole into the cave wall, hoping to find some other way out. They also continued to meditate to save energy, as well as to avoid thinking about food. Finally, British divers who had left from the cave's entrance three hours before made contact with the boys.

The first attempts to find and save the group were slowed by surging water levels and strong currents, and no contact could be made for more than a week. The cave rescue effort expanded into a huge operation fueled by intense public interest on a global scale. It ended up involving international rescue teams.

On July 2, after making their way through narrow passages and murky waters, British divers John Volanthen and Rick Stanton discovered the group alive but stranded on an elevated rock about four kilometers (or 2.5 miles) from the mouth of the cave.

Rescue organizers then went back and forth about the various options to get the group out intact. Should they teach them basic underwater diving skills to allow their early rescue, bide their time until a new entrance to the cave was either found or drilled, or even wait for the floodwaters to fall back by the end of the monsoon season, which would only come several months later?

After days of pumping water out of the cave system and a welcome break from rain, the rescue teams hurried to get the group out of the cave before the next monsoon rain fell from the darkening sky. That was predicted to bring more downpours and forecast to start around July 11.

But between July 8 and 10, all 12 boys and their coach were rescued from the cave by an international team. The rescue effort depended on as many as 10,000 people, including more than 100 divers, dozens of rescue workers, representatives from 100 diverse governmental agencies, 900 police officers, and 2,000 soldiers. On top of those, ten police helicopters, seven ambulances, more than 700 diving cylinders, and the energy and equipment to constantly pump more than one billion liters of water out of the caves were all needed.

Surviving for that long (more than two weeks, remember?!) was only half the battle. Thai SEALs entered the cave to help as well as hang out with the boys while rescuers above ground planned how to get them out safely. Over the course of that tough three-day rescue mission, experienced divers fetched each player and finally their coach.

The arduous journey to the surface also required each of them to put on a full-face diving mask, to be tied between two divers, and to swim for hours through excruciating turns and ridiculously tight subterranean squeezes.

Thanks to the efforts of the Thai Navy SEALs, along with the international dive community completely behind them, all the boys and their coach lived to see the light of day again. They were able to return to their normal, healthy lives following the rescue, together with the knowledge that they'd made it through a life-threatening ordeal due to their individual and group strength.

Saman Kunan, a 37-year-old who was formerly a Royal Thai Navy SEAL, died when he ran out of air during one rescue attempt on July 6 while returning to a staging base in the cave after delivering bulky diving cylinders to the trapped group. One year later, in December 2019, rescue diver and Thai Navy SEAL Beirut Pakbara passed away from a blood infection that struck him during the operation.

*[Although it's always sad to hear about any valiant person passing away at an early age, it's also good to know that there are real heroes in this world who risk their own lives to help others in desperate need. And who are the Navy SEALs anyway? Where do they come from? Perhaps they're named in part after those forever frolicking marine mammals called seals, but there's so much more.

In the 1960s, during the so-called Vietnam War, the U.S. military began to train special soldiers who could move around secretly in small teams and complete special military missions. This was the way the Navy SEALs started.

You need to know that any person who wants to become a SEAL must first join the Navy. Then they must pass some tough tests to be sure they're ready for BUD/S training which is a difficult camp where leaders decide who's really ready to be a Navy SEAL. They need to run through wet sand with all their clothes on, crawl through deep mud, and carry heavy rubber boats. It's not exactly a piece of cake.

They must do lots of situps and pushups and plenty of running. On most normal days, they get extraordinarily little sleep, and on top of that, have to swim far out in the ocean, and hold their breath underwater for a long time. Not only must their bodies be strong, but their minds as well. They have to be able to keep going and going, even when their bodies and minds desperately want to give up.

People who want to become Navy SEALs spend many years training before they even get into BUD/S Training. That's because it's so tough that many of them simply aren't able to finish. It doesn't mean that they're weak—it only means that it's a terrific challenge to finally become a Navy SEAL.

At the end of boot camp, SEALs start other kinds of training, such as learning how to scuba dive underwater, and how to parachute out of airplanes that fly ridiculously high. They also learn how to do some cool stuff, like shoot guns and set off bombs. The word SEAL is a combination of the words "sea," "air," and "land"—all together. This means a SEAL needs to be able to move readily across the sea, air, and land to accomplish all their special missions.

SEAL training lasts for up to a year. But even when they're done, they never stop practicing, and then they practice some more. A Navy SEAL is never fully done—they need to constantly keep learning and improving (doesn't this sound kind of like you and your friends at school?).

At the end of their first training period, the trainees are given a gold badge that has a symbol of an eagle on it, which they then pin to their Navy uniform. It's a really exciting and rewarding day for everybody, because they've worked so hard and long to reach their lofty goals.

Once a Navy SEAL completes her or his training, they're assigned to a team. That team may live anywhere in the world because their mission may take place anywhere around the globe. Thus, they need to be close and ready whenever and wherever they're needed.

When a mission takes place, the Navy SEALs might arrive there by plane, where they need to parachute down, or it could be by boat or helicopter, or even by submarine, if they're scuba swimming to their mission. They wear camouflage clothes depending on where the missions are, since it may be in the desert or the jungle, or even in the middle of a big city.

The Navy SEALs have assisted in many past wars and are active today in locations like the Middle East. Their mission could be to capture an enemy, or to rescue someone who's been kidnapped (like those adventures you read about before). SEALs are extremely fast and skilled at what they do and can get in and out of places as rapidly as anybody in town.

During one specific mission in the past, their job was to stop modern-day pirates who'd captured a large ship, including all its crew. On another mission, they rescued soldiers who'd been captured by the enemy.

Sometimes, the Navy SEALs have to sacrifice their own lives when they go on such dangerous missions. In 2005, during the Afghanistan War, a 4-man SEAL team landed by helicopter in an enemy area. Their job was to capture a dangerous Taliban leader. The members of the team were Lieutenant Michael Murphy, along with Petty Officers Marcus Luttrell, Danny Dietz, and Matt Axelson.

While trying to sneak through enemy territory, the team met a boy and his father herding goats. The team decided to leave them alone. But just after they let them go, the father alerted the Enemy, and the team was quickly under attack from all sides. The SEALs fought for a lengthy battle, trying their best to survive. But in the end, only Luttrell was left alive.

Of course, Marcus was strong, and he kept fighting and running until he was finally sheltered by a friendly villager who lived nearby. Many times, it's not easy to know who's a friend or enemy in a war. Yet this family took care of Marcus until a Navy helicopter came and took him away to safety.

After arriving home, Marcus decided to draft a book about the battle he faced with his tough team. He called it "Lone Survivor." Navy SEALs are in many ways regular people who want to make changes in the world while serving their country. Their job is surely never easy, but they practice long and hard to be extremely good at what they do.

What about spending some time thinking about what you can do to improve yourself, just like a Navy SEAL? Obviously, you don't necessarily have to become a SEAL to make yourself stronger or get better at something.

It might just be playing outside more, instead of watching TV, or riding your bike, or swimming, or doing something kind for someone else—a person you know, or maybe you don't know at all.

You too can have the spirit of a Navy SEAL, that's to achieve great things even when they take loads of time, hard work, and tons of practice. Surely, you'll have some unforgettable adventures along the way as well.

CHAPTER 12:

BARELY BACK FROM
THE MOON ON APOLLO 13

To date, no living humans have been as far into space as the crew of Apollo 13. The crew on that spacecraft followed a path that took them 248,655 miles from Earth before they swung back down this way for a most miraculous landing.

Yet the crew never made it to the surface of the moon. That was their original destination. Instead, Jim Lovell, Jack Swigert, and Fred Hayse faced a problem that might've killed them all: some defective wiring ignited an oxygen tank, which then blew out part of the spaceship.

The third mission that was planned by the U.S. to put astronauts on the Moon was called Apollo 13. It took off on April 11, 1970. The mission almost ended in total tragedy.

There was an explosion and then a power failure that partly disabled the spacecraft's command module, Odyssey, as it neared the Moon. But the astronauts were able to use their lunar module, Aquarius, as a temporary lifeboat, and finally returned safely to Earth.

Who were the Apollo 13 astronauts? They were spacecraft commander James A. Lovell, Jr., lunar module pilot Fred Haise, Jr., and command module pilot John L. Swigert, Jr. (it almost seemed like NASA had a requirement that you had to be a "Junior" to fly on this space mission!).

Swigert took the place of scheduled pilot Ken Mattingly since Ken was exposed to a sickness called measles a few days before the launch. The Saturn V launch vehicle of Apollo 13 lifted off from Cape Kennedy, Florida, at 2:13 PM on April 11, 1970.

The spacecraft was first sent into the Earth's orbit, then boosted into a trajectory around the Moon by the third stage of the Saturn rocket. Stuff like the transposition and docking of Odyssey and Aquarius were conducted.

In the early evening, Apollo 13 was cruising toward the Moon on a path so precise that the first planned course adjustment could be canceled. Later, the craft was changed to something called a "non-free return" trajectory to attempt a landing in the Moon's Fra Mauro region.

This transfer signified that, if no other propulsive maneuver was made during the flight, then Apollo 13 would swing around the Moon and return toward Earth but would miss the astronauts' home planet by about 2,950 miles. That seems like a pretty big miss to us.

Sunday, April 12, passed without any problem. But early on the evening of Monday, April 13, almost 56 hours after the flight began, Lovell and Haise entered Aquarius to begin checking systems.

Suddenly, they heard a loud bang, and all electrical power failed in Odyssey. The three astronauts quickly got together in Odyssey to try to find out what happened. Finding problems in the main electrical systems, Haise and Lovell radioed Mission Control in Houston, Texas, with a scary message. It went like this:

Haise: Okay, Houston—

Lovell: I believe we've had a problem here.

Mission Control: This is Houston. Say again, please.

Lovell: Houston, we've had a problem. We've had a Main B Bus Undervolt.

To make a long story short, a routine flight had quickly become one of the most exciting episodes in space history.

Much later, they found that the bang was an oxygen-tank explosion in Odyssey's service module.

This caused an oxygen shortage which made breathing hard. It also disabled the three fuel cells that normally provided electricity and drinking water for the command module.

The safety of the astronauts caused anxiety that was felt all around the world. Millions of people stayed glued to their TV and radio sets as the dangerous journey played itself out.

Plans for a lunar landing were abandoned, and the astronauts transferred into the lunar module, Aquarius. It had enough power, oxygen, and water to keep them alive while the hobbled spacecraft swung around the Moon and returned towards Earth.

The systems on the Odyssey - the only module that could reenter Earth's atmosphere - were turned off to save emergency battery power.

Early in the morning on Tuesday, April 14, the spacecraft came closer to the Moon, and Aquarius's engine was fired to put it into a free-return trajectory. That meant it should be able to return to Earth, but nobody knew for sure.

Then, Apollo 13 lost radio contact with Earth as it passed behind the Moon. But that was expected. As the craft's path took it higher above the Moon than other Apollo missions, Apollo 13 broke the record for the flight farthest from Earth: 248,655 miles.

Communication was restored when the craft came out from behind the Moon. Around that time, Saturn's third stage had been discarded and crashed into the Moon, according to plan, providing a kind of fake moonquake for scientists to study.

Two hours later, Aquarius's engine was fired again to increase the craft's speed and reduce its flight time by 10 hours. That was supposed to guarantee a splashdown in the Pacific Ocean, somewhere south of the island of Samoa.

Meanwhile, on board the spacecraft, the amount of oxygen continued to be sufficient, as did the cooling water.

The astronauts cut their consumption of drinking water to six measly ounces per day, and their use of precious electricity by 80 percent. However, carbon dioxide levels in the lunar module started to rise to risky levels.

The craft's lithium hydroxide absorbers (needed to remove carbon dioxide from the air) had become saturated.

The air purifiers in the command module didn't fit the Aquarius. As a result, NASA engineers had to quickly improvise a purification system.

They radioed the astronauts with detailed instructions on how to put together a new purification system from materials found on the spacecraft, including stuff like cardboard, plastic bags, and duct tape (the same kind of tape you use to hold your hockey stick together or stick up some posters on your wall).

The quickly designed system worked well and kept the carbon dioxide content of the air far below hazardous levels for the rest of the mission.

One more course correction was made on the morning of Wednesday, April 15. The change was successful, and the flight continued. Meanwhile, the temperature inside the lunar module dropped to 38 °F. The cold, exhausted astronauts slept badly, but they had received instructions on spacecraft separation and reentry maneuvers they would soon need to perform upon their critical approach to Earth.

Preparing to reenter Earth's atmosphere, the astronauts first got rid of the service module, taking vital photos of the damaged section as it separated.

Then, they made their way into the command module and discarded the lifesaving Aquarius, which couldn't make it back to Earth either.

The command module did enter the Earth's atmosphere without burning or breaking up. It splashed down in the ocean and was on target on April 17; 142 hours, 54 minutes, and 41 seconds after the mission started.

A recovery team from the aircraft carrier USS Iwo Jima was ready to pick up the heroic astronauts. Despite being a bit tired, they were flown immediately to Hawaii to meet their families.

President Richard Nixon was on his way to visit the Apollo 13 crew when he stopped in the city of Houston to award the

Presidential Medal of Freedom, the nation's highest civilian award, to the whole Mission Control team.

Even though the lunar module had been a safe place for the astronauts in space, the craft couldn't survive atmospheric re-entry.

Thus, the crew moved back into the damaged command module before miraculously making it to the ground (in fact, the ocean). All were unharmed, although Hayse was pretty thirsty - in fact, he was seriously dehydrated.

As a result of the near-disaster, NASA appointed a review board. It was led by Edgar M. Cortright, director of Langley Research Center, to investigate the Apollo 13 accident.

After two months of detailed study, the board traced the root cause of the explosion to two protective thermostatic switches in an oxygen-tank heater assembly. They were found to be inadequate.

Further Apollo flights were delayed until 1971 so that changes could be made to prevent similar incidents. In 1995, Apollo 13, a feature-length motion picture of the mission was launched. The Hollywood blockbuster starred actor Tom Hanks (ask your parents about him!).

More amazingly, after the success of this movie in '95, Hanks himself spent four full years helping produce another film in the Imax format, which permitted viewers like you and your pals to feel like you were in that cramped spaceship! In the same film, you could also sense that you were on the moon's actual surface, right alongside Neil Armstrong and Buzz Aldrin (not Lightyear!).

Those space missions were among the greatest adventures ever experienced by anyone.

Between 1969 and 1972, only a dozen men flew hundreds of thousands of miles across space to land on the Moon. For the first and only time in the history of humanity, people walked on another world.

Then these out-of-this-world experiences were shared with moviegoers. We need to give some special thanks to the astronautical fixations of Hollywood's biggest spaceflight enthusiast, Tom Hanks.

The star wrote, narrated, and produced a whopping 3D spectacular called "Magnificent Desolation: Walking on the Moon 3D", which was specially filmed for Imax theaters.

The aim of this lavish production was simple, according to Tom: "It's to give the audience a never-before-seen chance to stand on the Moon right next to Neil, right next to Buzz."

At one point, using actual footage of the moon landings, audiences "find themselves" together with Neil Armstrong and Buzz Aldrin inside the cramped cabin of Apollo 11's Eagle Lander, the first lunar module to touch down on the moon.

On another, they're on a lunar rover vehicle when it zips by craters and skims over strange rocks.

The film took four years to make and could clearly be traced to Hanks's lead role as astronaut Jim Lovell in Ron Howard's film, Apollo 13. As you now know, it dramatized the story of the lunar mission that was wrecked by an exploding fuel tank. It was a great film, says Hanks, and was only missing a real sense of actually placing the viewer on the Moon's surface.

"What was still lacking was the tactile experience of going to the Moon; what the actual vista looks like, how the Sea of Tranquility goes off into infinity," added Hanks. "Our aim, with this film, is to bring along anyone who wants to take that giant leap for themselves," the movie star enthused.

It's nice that we could take that adventuresome leap without leaving the comfort of our cinema seats!

CHAPTER 13:

A PERSON NAMED BLACKJACK, ALONE ON AN ISLAND

Alaska native Ada Blackjack was a member of the Indigenous Inupiat people. Canadians Vilhjalmur Stefansson and Allan Crawford hired her to join them on an expedition to the Wrangel Islands—now considered part of Russian territory. The goal was to claim them in the name of Canada, and Blackjack acted as the seamstress and cook for the expedition (among other vital duties).

Blackjack - her family name (before she was married) was Ada Deletuk -was born in 1898 in Spruce Creek, Alaska. It was a remote settlement north of the Arctic circle near the gold rush town of Nome. History doesn't pay too much attention to her, although Jennifer Niven's 2004 biography, Ada Blackjack: A True Story of Survival in the Arctic, encompassed a complete picture of her life.

While Blackjack was Inupiat, she wasn't really raised with any knowledge of hunting, or wilderness survival. Rather, she was brought up by Methodist missionaries who taught her enough English to be able to study the bible. They instructed her in housekeeping, sewing, and cooking "white people" food.

At the tender age of 16, she married Jack Blackjack, a local dog musher, and together they had three children - two of them died - before Jack left Ada all alone on the Seward Peninsula in 1921. After being abandoned, Blackjack walked 40 miles back to Nome with her five-year-old son, Bennett. When he was simply too tired to walk, she carried him.

The boy suffered from tuberculosis (TB) and poor health in general. Blackjack didn't have the cash to care for him properly. Destitute, she placed Bennett in a local orphanage, promising that she'd find a way to make enough money to bring him back home.

It was at that time Blackjack heard of an expedition heading for Wrangel Island: they were seeking an Alaska Native tailor who spoke some English. The expedition, organized by the energetic Arctic explorer Vilhjalmur Stefansson, was really an ill-conceived venture.

Using the power of his celebrity as a seasoned explorer, Stefansson assembled a team of four enthusiastic young men - Allan Crawford, 20, Lorne Knight, 28, Fred Maurer, 28, and Milton Galle, 19 - to claim Wrangel Island for the British Empire—although England had never shown the least interest in wanting it before.

Though Stefansson picked his own team, as well as funding the mission, he never had any plan to actually join the party himself. He sent his badly inexperienced team to the north with only six months of supplies and some weak assurances that "the friendly

Arctic" would yield ample animals to supplement their goods until a ship picked them up the next year.

Blackjack had plenty of doubt about shipping out with an expedition of four young men, especially as she was initially told she'd be just one of many indigenous Alaskans in the group. But the part-time jobs sewing and housekeeping that she could pick up in Nome were never going to suffice to bring Bennett home. The Wrangel Island expedition promised a salary of $50 a month - money that to Blackjack was an other-worldly sum.

Even when the rest of the Inuits who were hired pulled out, Blackjack boarded the Silver Wave together with Crawford, Knight, Maurer, Galle, and the ship's cat, Victoria, on September 9, 1921. The first year on Wrangel Island lived up to Stefansson's promises. When summer came to an end though, the once-abundant game disappeared while the pack ice closed in. There was no sign of any ship.

Of course, the party didn't know, but the Teddy Bear - the ship meant to pick them up - was forced to turn around due to impenetrable ice. As the weather took a turn for the worst, the group had to face the reality that their limited stores had to last another year.

Five members of the expedition were left on the island on September 16, 1921, to make a territorial claim. By the beginning of 1923, the situation had turned dire: the party was starving, and Knight was extremely ill with undiagnosed scurvy. On January 28, 1923, Crawford, Maurer, and Galle made the decision to leave Blackjack to care for the seriously sick Knight. They set out on foot across the ice to Siberia in search of help and were never seen again.

For six months, Blackjack was alone with Knight. She served as "doctor, nurse, companion, servant, and huntswoman in one," said the Los Angeles Times in 1924. "Ada was woodsman, too." Sadly, the dying man projected the anger he felt over his helplessness onto her. He criticized her constantly for not taking better care of him.

Blackjack couldn't allow his criticism to slow her down, but she came clean in her diary: "He never stop and think how much its hard for women to take four mans place, to wood work and to hund for something to eat for him and do waiting to his bed and take the shiad [shit] out for him."

When Knight passed away, Blackjack even recorded the event on Galle's typewriter in this way:

> "The daid of Mr. Knights death
> He died on June 23rd.

I dont know what time he died though
Anyway I write the daid. Just to
let Mr Steffansom know what month he
died and what daid of the month.

written by Mrs. Ada B, Jack."

After Knight's passing, Blackjack refused to feel completely down. Instead, she focused on the task of surviving so she could be reunited with her son. She didn't have the emotional or physical strength to bury Knight's body, so she left him resting on his bed inside his sleeping bag while setting up a barricade of boxes to protect his body from the wild animals that visited.

Jennifer Niven later wrote in her biography on Ada Blackjack, she "moved into the storage tent to escape the smell of decay... she drove driftwood into the ground to bolster the tattered walls and ceiling of the tent. She built a cupboard out of boxes, which she placed at the entrance, and in this she stored her field glasses and ammunition."

Even more important was that Blackjack built a gun rack above her bed so that she wouldn't be too surprised if polar bears got a bit too close to her camp.

For three months, Blackjack was totally alone. She figured out how to set traps to attract white foxes, taught herself to shoot birds, created a platform above her shelter so she could spy polar bears in the distance, and even fashioned a skin boat from driftwood and stretched canvas after the one first brought to the island was taken away by a storm.

She even messed around with the expedition's photography equipment and succeeded in taking pictures of herself standing outside the camp. On August 20, 1923, nearly two years after first landing on Wrangel Island, the schooner Donaldson showed up on the horizon to rescue the resilient seamstress. She was surviving very well on her own.

"Blackjack," one of the crew members wrote, "mastered her environment so far that it seems likely she could have lived there another year, although the isolation would have been a dreadful experience." News of the expedition's tragic end was broadcast, leaving Blackjack in the middle of a flurry of media attention. She was recognized by some as a hero and praised her for her courage.

The humble woman avoided the spotlight and titles, insisting that she was just a mother who needed to get home to her son. Ada was finally reunited with Bennett and took her payment - less than she'd been promised - from her time on Wrangel Island to get treatment for his TB in a Seattle hospital.

Later, she had a second son named Billy, and went back to live in Alaska. Even though this seemed to be a kind of happy ending, Blackjack's remaining years were shaded with sadness and poverty. Stefansson and others managed to profit from the tragic expedition story, but Blackjack never saw any of that money.

Later people spoke out against her Character, even claiming that she had refused to take care of Knight. On the other hand, Knight's family "eventually vindicated her after meeting with her and issuing a statement that Blackjack had done everything possible to save their son's life."

Bennett's health never really recovered. He died from a stroke in 1972 at age 58. Blackjack joined her son about 10 years later, passing away in a nursing home in Palmer, Alaska, at the age of 85. She was buried at her son Bennett's side.

CHAPTER 14:

SHACKLETON'S JOURNEY TO THE END OF THE EARTH

It seems like many of the greatest adventure stories we ever hear deal with similar emotions: people's fear of the unknown, and of course the curse of loneliness, as well as the need to be brave and inventive, and persist in the face of all odds, in the most dangerous situations.

But why would anybody want to make the extreme effort to cross the entire continent of Antarctica, probably the coldest and clearly the southernmost in the world? After all, there's nothing there but ice and snow and bitter wind (well, there are in fact a lot of super-cute penguins). There's no TV or any video games or social media channels, or hamburgers and fries for that matter - at least not back in 1914 when perhaps the grandest adventure you'll ever hear about happened.

There was once an Englishman named Ernest Shackleton, and he happened to be quite competitive. Is competition really the best reason to create adventures? Maybe not, but it certainly drives people to do insane things (in the eyes of others, that is), as you'll soon find out in the last part, Chapter 16, of this book.

Shackleton was pushed to bigger and better things by one of his most direct competitors - a Norwegian man named Roald Amundsen. Shortly before his own exciting expedition, this is what Ernest said: "After the conquest of the South Pole by Amundsen who, by a narrow margin of days only, was in advance of the British Expedition under Scott, there remained but one great main object of Antarctic journeying - the crossing of the South Polar continent, from sea to sea."

So, this was what led to the Imperial Trans-Antarctica expedition from 1914 to 1917. The goal was ambitious – even crazy - considering that only 10 men had ever stood at the South Pole before that, and five of those died on the way back. The story that unfolds was way beyond any expectations, and completely different from the original plan.

Simply speaking, it's one of the most amazing adventure stories of all time. It was remarkable even for an era and a faraway, hostile place that already had far more than its share of incredible stories of heroes and their fortitude in the face of the toughest hardships.

The idea was to cross the continent of Antarctica from one coast to the other, passing by the South Pole. But in this event, the main expedition never truly set foot on the Antarctic continent. The expedition did manage to survive the complete loss of their ship in the midst of the Antarctic pack ice. At that time, there was no way to contact the outside world, or more importantly, to be rescued.

Shackleton started to plan his next Antarctica Journey as soon as he returned from the Nimrod Expedition from 1907 to 1909. He was sure that others would soon reach the South Pole where he had failed, although he'd come so close. Crossing the Antarctic continent from coast to coast via the South Pole was a distance of 1,800 miles. It was certainly a long way, but not really much further than a "there-and-back" journey to the pole.

Ernest planned to set out from the Weddell Sea region (located to the south of South America) and cross a region of Antarctica that had never been explored, then go to the pole, and lastly to the Ross Sea and McMurdo Sound area (located south of New Zealand).

Typically, on such trips, the exploratory part of the expedition (which would generate international attention) was only a small part of a whole. Other scientific and exploratory sledding excursions were planned for groups leaving from the main base, plus another party who were supposed to stay at the base to conduct scientific work.

Another group would be needed to set out from the Ross Sea region in order to lay depots for the Trans-Antarctic party to use later on their journey to the coast from the pole. They would be on a second ship.

The ship used for the journey to the Weddell Sea was freshly built in a Norwegian shipyard and was meant for tourist cruises around the Arctic. She was called the Endurance. The ship that would take the Ross Sea party was named the Aurora, bought from Douglas Mawson, which he used on his Antarctic journey from 1911 to 1914.

The expedition was flooded with applications from volunteers wanting to join, despite (or perhaps because of) the sad end for Robert Scott and his team after they reached the South Pole two years earlier.

You can find a much-publicized newspaper ad which Shackleton supposedly placed before the grand expedition (although no copy has ever been found in any archive). It read:

"MEN WANTED: FOR HAZARDOUS JOURNEY. SMALL WAGES, BITTER COLD, LONG MONTHS OF COMPLETE DARKNESS, CONSTANT DANGER, SAFE RETURN DOUBTFUL. HONOUR AND RECOGNITION IN CASE OF SUCCESS. SIR ERNEST SHACKLETON"

(We're not so sure about you, but we guess that in this day and age, not many people would actually jump at this unique opportunity!)

Getting enough money for such a big journey would always be a problem. Shackleton himself did most of the recruiting and preparation for the Endurance's departure, while also desperately fighting to find more cash. If money didn't roll in, the expedition might never take place at all. Eventually, some funding was found, and near the end of July 1914, things were almost ready.

The dark clouds of World War I were also beginning to form. The Endurance laid at anchor off Southend on August 4, 1914, when Shackleton saw in a daily newspaper the government order for general mobilization of troops and supplies along with calls for volunteer soldiers.

He immediately went to his ship, called for all hands on deck, and told them that he'd send a telegram to the Admiralty announcing his offer of the ships, supplies, and services to their country if war broke out.

Only one hour after sending the telegram, Shackleton got a single word reply from the Admiralty: "Proceed." Within two hours, another arrived from Winston Churchill: he thanked them for their offer but wanted the expedition to go forward. At midnight exactly, war did break out.

On August 8, the Endurance sailed for the Antarctic, first to Buenos Aires, and then to the sub-Antarctic Island of South Georgia where there was a Norwegian whaling station. People believed the war would be done within six months, so when it was time to leave for the south, they departed with no regrets.

November 5, 1914: they arrived at South Georgia. Shackleton picked the brains of the whaling captains on the conditions between there and the Weddell Sea. They indicated that it was an especially heavy-ice year. The initial plan was to spend only a few days collecting stores, but the Endurance stayed in South Georgia for a full month to give the ice further south time to break up.

That month allowed time for bonds of friendship and mutual respect to be strengthened between the crew of the Endurance and the Norwegian whalers. Those bonds were to prove extremely useful a time later to both Shackleton and his hardy men.

The Weddell Sea was infamous for being particularly ice-bound even in the best of times. Thus, the Endurance left with a deck-load of coal plus the normal stores. That would help with the extra load on the engines when it came to making it through the pack ice in the Weddell Sea to the Antarctic continent and beyond.

Extra clothes and stores were brought from South Georgia in case the Endurance needed to winter in the ice if it got stuck in the Weddell Sea as it froze and was unable to reach the continent first. They departed from South Georgia on December 5, 1914.

The Endurance fought its way through a thousand miles of pack ice over a period of six weeks, and was a hundred miles (equal to one day's sail) from her destination, when on the January 18, 1915, at 76°34'S (the precise coordinates on the map, in case you're interested), the ice closed in all around the wooden ship. The temperature was dropping dramatically and glued together all the loose ice that surrounded the ship. The ship's storekeeper wrote that she was "like an almond in a piece of toffee." A sweet image, but not so nice for those on board.

On the one hand, this wasn't totally unexpected. It happened to ships in the Arctic and Antarctic many times, but it was a big setback. For Shackleton, the disappointment was indeed bitter. He was already 40 years old; his country was at war, the expedition had already taken vast amounts of effort, energy, and money to prepare, and he was unlikely to have this chance again.

Yet his men still looked up to "the Boss" as they called him. This unique group of Royal Naval sailors, rough trawler hands, along with recent Cambridge University graduates, among others, depended on the man who had brought them to this place, and into the heart of this very unfortunate situation.

The ship drifted to the Southwest, carried by the ice. Several tries were made to free the ship when cracks appeared in the nearby ice, but it was no use. The ice packed around the ship was thick and solid. Workers with heavy ice chisels and iron bars tried to break up the ice near the ship, yet running the ship at full speed ahead had no effect at all. They continued to drift.

At the end of February, temperatures had plummeted and were regularly minus 20°C. The ship was obviously frozen in for the winter. The two main concerns were: where would the drifting ice lead them, and would it even be possible to break out in the spring season?

The sides of the ship were kept clear so that if the ice began to press together, hopefully the Endurance would be able to move above the ice, and ride on it - instead of being crushed without hope.

This possibility hadn't been planned for, and the men were quickly frustrated and restless. However, football and hockey games were frequent features on the sea ice, at least until the heavy darkness of the Antarctic winter descended. Finally, the glow of sunrise came again in early July, signaling the return of the sun and daylight. But the weather was never completely hospitable: regular blizzards and low temperatures persisted. Most worrisome of all was the constant pressure from the pack ice: floes began to "raft" or pass over each other.

Everybody was aware that one of two things would happen: either the pack ice would thaw out, break up, and disperse in the spring, and thus free the ship. Or even more ice would pile up, and then be pushed by the powerful effects of wind and tide over hundreds of miles of sea. Finally, it would seize the ship and crush it - like a tiny toy in a pressing vice.

The crew went out to look for fresh meat for the dogs and themselves. They found it in the form of seals and penguins. But they were still in low supply since they basically disappeared at the start of winter, even though a few had been taken at the end of September.

On October 23, 1915, their position was 69°11'S, longitude 51°5'W.

The Endurance continued to be under heavy pressure from the ice and wasn't sitting in a good position. Instead of being free to slip upwards with the increasing pressure, the ice had a firm hold on the sensitive ship.

The first sign of real damage was to the sternpost: it twisted, and the planking buckled in the same area. Then the ship sprang a leak. The bilge pumps were fired up, and at first the leak was kept under control.

On October 27, Shackleton penned in his log, "The position was lat. 69°5'S, long. 51°30'W. The temperature was -8.5°F, a gentle southerly breeze was blowing, and the sun shone in a cloudless sky. After long months of ceaseless anxiety and strain, after times when hope beat high, and times when the outlook was black indeed, we have been compelled to abandon the ship, which is crushed beyond all hope of ever being righted. We are alive and well, and we have stores and equipment for the task that lies before us. The task is to reach land with all the members of the Expedition. It is hard to write what I feel."

At that point, the Endurance had drifted at least 1,186 miles since it first got stuck in the ice 281 days before. She was 346 miles from Paulet Island, the nearest point where there existed any possibility of finding food and shelter. Shackleton ordered the boats, gear, provisions, and sledges all lowered onto the ice.

The men set up five tents 100 yards from the ship but were quickly forced to move as a ridge of pressure started to split the ice beneath them. "Ocean Camp" was established on a thick, heavy floe of ice one and a half miles from what was quickly becoming the wreck of the much-loved Endurance.

The ship finally broke up completely and sank slowly below the ice and waters of the Weddell Sea on November 21, 1915. The men saved as many supplies as possible (including Frank

Hurley's precious photo archive) before she disappeared, down to a watery grave.

The expedition's 28 members were now secluded on the drifting pack ice - hundreds of miles from any land, with no ship, no way to communicate with the outside world, and with very slim supplies. What was even worse: the ice itself was starting to break up as the Antarctic spring started. On December 20, Shackleton decided that it was time to give up their camp and march west to where they thought the nearest land was, namely Paulet Island.

The three lifeboats named after patrons of the expedition (who'd donated funds) stood by. Two of those were then hauled in relays, the James Caird, and the Dudley Docker. The third boat, the Stancomb Wills, was left behind. If the ice suddenly started to disappear beneath them, the men would resort to these 20-foot boats to survive.

Led by Frank Wild, some of the crew went back to the area where the Endurance had rested to retrieve the Stancomb Wills. That would give them more space and prove to be a wise decision in the months to come.

All men were forced into the boats by the thinning, increasingly fragile ice on April 9, 1916, and They made their way across a stretch of open water. By evening, they were able once again to haul the boats onto a large ice floe and set up their tents. (The next time you go camping with family or friends, imagine how it must be to pitch your tent on moving ice, and then get a good night's rest!)

The fact that the crew kept going at this time was a true tribute to Shackleton's leadership skills, and his grasp of the critical need to keep up morale. The whole group was kept together in the monotonous yet strenuous task of pulling packed lifeboats across broken up and ridged ice floes—never knowing when one false step could send them tumbling into freezing waters.

It was then 14 months since the Endurance had become frozen in the ice, and almost five months since she had sunk, which marooned them all in an icy wilderness, absent of any features. On April 12, Shackleton found that instead of making substantial progress to the west, they had somehow traveled 30 miles to the east due to the drifting ice. (Just to remind you: GPS didn't exist yet!)

They did however spot Elephant Island, which was part of the South Shetlands group. They headed that way in seas that were by then mostly open for navigation. Overjoyed, they made landfall on Elephant Island. It had been 497 days since they had last set foot on land. (For those of you without a calculator, that's almost a year and a half!)

Their first landing place wasn't ideal by any means, but they soon found a better place to make camp at a place they called Point Wild. They named it after Frank Wild who'd gone down the coast to scout things out.

"As we clustered round the blubber stove, with the acrid smoke blowing in our faces, we were quite a cheerful company. Life was not so bad. We ate our evening meal while the snow drifted down from the surface of the glacier, and our chilled bodies grew warm," Shackleton wrote.

But Shackleton realized that if he wanted to arrange a rescue, he needed to travel to the nearest inhabited place which was the whaling station back on South Georgia - some 800 miles away — and across the world's stormiest stretch of ocean. They expected to face waves that were 50 feet from tip to trough, meaning from top to bottom (they called them "Cape Horn Rollers"), in only a 22-foot-long boat.

Their navigation was done using a basic instrument known as a sextant, along with a chronometer of unknown accuracy. In addition, they were dependent on sightings of the sun - that golden orb that could sometimes not even be seen for weeks in the cloudy weather typical of those far southern latitudes.

Shackleton selected Frank Wild to stay behind with the men on Elephant Island. He felt that Wild was the guy who could hold them together well. If there was no spring rescue, their instructions were to try to reach Deception Island, a place frequented by whalers and sealers. The lifeboat chosen for that journey was the trusty 'James Caird.'

That craft was made more seaworthy by the limited means available and fitted with a small cover to protect it against the weather and the sea. Launching her was a big adventure in itself. Many of the men got soaked to the bone, a serious problem in the cold climate, and with practically no facilities for drying their clothes out, and then managing to get warm again.

The party left behind on Elephant Island used the two remaining lifeboats to create a kind of hut. Turned upside down and placed on top of two low stone walls, they used fabric from the tents and sails as lining to keep the wind and weather out. The men were even able to make small celluloid windows from an old photo case, while a blubber stove provided heat and was also used as a cooker.

Conditions were terribly cramped, and food was always in short supply. Every day, the men felt pangs of hunger. One member of the party, Blackborow (who was just a boy who joined the ship as a stowaway in Buenos Aries - his companion had been hired but he hadn't) suffered from frostbitten toes. They had to be amputated by the party's surgeons by the little light that came from the blubber stove.

The James Caird set off on April 24, 1916, which the very last day before the ice pack closed in again around Elephant Island. It was a day of relative calm. The crew consisted of Shackleton, Worsley, Crean, McNeish, McCarthy, and Vincent. The expected journey time was one month. It would become one of the most amazing small boat voyages of all time.

The James Caird made progress, moving at a rate of 60 to 70 miles per day through rough seas. The ocean constantly came in, making everything wet, including the sleeping bags. It was hard to find any warmth at all. There were four sleeping bags made of reindeer hide which shed their hairs in the constant wetness, thus making them less effective while also clogging the pump needed to empty the sea water that spilled into the boat.

The boat was relatively light, so rocks and other ballast had been placed onboard in order to trim her (in other words, to find and maintain the best angle of the boat to help it cut through the water). But these objects had to be constantly moved around.

The weather got worse and worse, and soon they faced fierce storms. While the temperature dropped, ice developed on the outside of the boat from frozen sea spray - up to 15 inches deep on the deck. This made the boat much heavier and in turn affected the trim - thus more moving around of the rocks was required.

The men tried as much as they could to chip away the accumulated ice with any tools they could improvise, though the situation just grew worse. The last option was to throw precious items overboard in order to cut weight - the extra oars went into the sea and so did two sleeping bags that were totally soaked through - hard and heavy with ice.

At other times, they had to furiously bail water out of the boat for dear life. The only solace during this journey were the hot meals made every four hours by the light of a simple primus stove. At that point, they'd been drifting for some time under light sail, and held back by the sea anchor (a sea anchor is a kind of large canvas bag that acts to slow the boat and prevent it from being thrown around so violently during stormy seas) due to the roughness of the seas.

However, the sea anchor was suddenly lost as the boat fell dramatically into a large trough between big waves. The men then had to beat the canvas sails free of ice and set them once again to keep on course. Frostbite was beginning to affect all member's exposed fingers and hands in the shivering cold and constant wetness.

Navigation was also a problem due to the constantly overcast weather. On the seventh day at sea, a miraculous break in the clouds came. Worsley was able to take a reading from the sun, six days since his last observation. He calculated that they'd traveled around 380 miles and were then almost halfway to South Georgia.

The brief period of sun meant that the men were able to quickly spread their clothing and other gear over the boat deck and the mast to dry it out. The ice became less dense, and they occasionally were accompanied by wildlife, like porpoises, and tiny storm petrels. You wouldn't say that their spirits soared exactly, but there was a glimmer of some hope.

On May 5, the eleventh day way out at sea, the water became much worse. Shackleton was responsible for the tiller: "I called to the other men that the sky was clearing, and then a moment later I realized that what I had seen was not a rift in the clouds, but the white crest of an enormous wave. During twenty-six years' experience of the ocean in all its moods, I had not encountered a wave so gigantic.

It was a mighty upheaval of the ocean, a thing quite apart from the big white-capped seas that had been our tireless enemies for many days. I shouted, 'For God's sake, hold on! It's got us.' Then came a moment of suspense that seemed drawn out into hours. We felt our boat lifted and flung forward like a cork in breaking surf. We were in a seething chaos of tortured water.

But somehow the boat lived through it, half full of water, sagging to the dead weight and shuddering under the blow. We bailed with the energy of men fighting for life, flinging the water over the sides with every receptacle that came to our hands, and after ten minutes of uncertainty, we felt the boat renew her life beneath us," Ernest exclaimed.

On May 7, Worsley was able to take another navigational reading and calculated that they weren't more than a hundred miles from the northwest part of South Georgia. Another two days, and if they had the wind with them, they should have the island in sight.

The morning of May 8 came, and they began to see kelp floating in the sea. Then some sea birds winged by, and just after noon, they caught a glimpse of South Georgia, only fourteen days after leaving Elephant Island. That was about half as long as they expected the journey to last.

But landing the boat was a much less than straightforward deal: reefs (shallow rocks just below the sea surface) stretched all along the coast where they were, and great waves crashed over them. The rocky coast in many places dropped steeply into the sea. Despite being so close, in addition to running out of fresh water to drink, they had no choice: wait for the next morning to break before trying to land on the shore.

The morning brought a substantial change in the wind, and a terrible storm reared up. The 'James Caird' was tossed about on the precipitous waves, and when the light broke, somehow, they were out of sight of land once more. They made their way back to South Georgia a bit after noon. But again, it was only a hostile coast of huge breakers and sheer cliffs that greeted them.

The day wore on, and there seemed less and less hope. But later in the evening, the wind shifted direction again and then began to die down. By the morning of May 10, there was little wind, and they were able to look better for a landing place. But rocky reefs and breaking waves denied their every attempt.

They finally found a likely bay in which to land, but they were suddenly blown out to sea again by a change in the wind. Darkness fell, and they were finally able to enter a small cove fronted by a reef. They had to take in the oars to pass through. But at long last, carried forward by the swell, the 'James Caird' could land on a South Georgia beach at King Haakon Bay.

How had they made it alive? Thanks in part to Shackleton's leadership, and the incredible navigational skills of New Zealander Frank Worsley who'd only been able to take sightings of the sun four times: on April 26, and May 3, 4, and 7. All the rest had been what's called "dead reckoning": keeping on the same straight line with the same heading.

If they'd failed to land, the boat would have been swept onwards and surely lost in the middle of the frigid and vast Atlantic Ocean. Then no rescue party would've ever set out for the men left behind on Elephant Island.

But wait - there was still one more major obstacle to overcome. The crew of six on the James Caird had landed 22 miles from the Stromness whaling station - as the crow flies (in other words, in a straight line). To get there, they had to go across the spiny backbone of mountains that ran the length of South Georgia, a journey that nobody had ever completed. The map showed the area only as a big blank space.

At that moment, McNeish and Vincent were simply too weak to attempt the Journey, so Shackleton left them with McCarthy to care for them. On May 15, Shackleton, Crean, and Worsley set out to cross the mountains and walk to the whaling station: they crossed glistening glaciers, icy slopes, and snowy fields. At a height of 4,500 feet, they looked back and saw the fog closing in fast behind them.

Night was falling fast, and they carried no tent or sleeping bags. They had no choice but to descend to a lower altitude. They slid scarily down a snowy slope in a matter of minutes, losing 900 feet in the process. They were only able to have a hot meal with two of them protecting the cooker from the wind.

Darkness did descend, but they carried on walking. Soon a full moon appeared to light their way. They climbed again and ate another hot meal to renew some of their energy. They were able to make out an island in the distance that they recognized but realized then that they'd gone in the wrong Direction. They had to retrace their steps.

At 5:00 am., they sat down exhausted in the quiet space under a large rock and wrapped their arms around each Other, trying to keep warm. Worsley and Crean fell asleep, but Shackleton knew that if he did the same, they might never wake up again. He shook them awake five minutes later, telling them they'd slept for half an hour. Once again, dragging their frigid feet, they set off.

There was only one more ridge of jagged peaks between them and Stromness, and they managed to find a gap to go through.

At 6:30 am., Shackleton stood on a ridge he'd climbed to get a better look at the land below, and he could swear he heard the sound of a steam whistle calling the men of the whaling station out of their beds.

Returning to Worsley and Crean, he told them to watch for 7 o'clock - this would be when the whalers were called to work. And wouldn't you know, the whistle sounded right on time. The three men surely had never heard a more welcome sound in all their lives.

The three walked down to 2,000 feet above sea level. They came upon a sheet of steep ice. But two hours later, they'd cut steps and roped down another 500 feet. Lastly, a slippery slide down another slope put them at 1,500 feet above sea level on a plateau.

They still had some distance to go before reaching the whaling station. The going was less than easy, and they still had some tough climbing to do to get over ridges between them and their goal. But their newfound purpose and closeness carried them on.

At 1:30 pm., they scrambled over the final ridge and saw a small whaling boat entering the bay some 2,500 feet below. They hurried as fast as their pained bodies would allow, and then spotted a sailing ship lying at a wharf. Tiny figures were seen wandering about, and then finally they sighted the whaling factory. The men paused, shook hands, and congratulated each other on somehow accomplishing their heroic journey - alive.

But the only way down seemed to be along a stream flowing rapidly to the sea below. So they went down through the icy water, soaked to their waists, shivering cold and tired. Then they heard the unwelcome sound of a rushing waterfall. The stream went over a 30-foot fall with seemingly impassable ice-cliffs on both sides.

Since they were simply too tired to look for another way down, they agreed that the only way forward was through the waterfall itself. They fastened their rope around a rock and slowly lowered Crean, the heaviest of the three, into the waterfall.

He completely disappeared but came out at the bottom gasping for air. Shackleton went next, and Worsley, the most agile member of the party, went last. They'd dropped the logbook, adze, and cooker before going over the edge, and once they were on solid ground, the items were retrieved. In the end, those were the only items brought safely out of the Antarctic.

The whaling station lay just a tantalizing mile and a half away. They tried to smarten themselves up a bit before entering the station. But their beards were too long and scraggly, their hair was impossibly matted, their clothes were ripped and stained - they hadn't been cleaned in a year.

At 3 o'clock in the afternoon on May 20, 1916, they arrived at the outskirts of the Stromness whaling station. When they approached the station itself, two small boys met them. Shackleton asked them kindly where the manager's house was, but they didn't answer. They just turned and ran away from them as fast as they could.

To make a long story short, as people sometimes say, Shackleton and his comrades had made it alive to the whaling station where they were soon welcomed with open arms. After building back some of their strength, they returned to save the other members of their party, first on the other side of South Georgia, and finally, after four excruciating tries, the other men stranded on Elephant Island.

"We had entered a year and a half before with well-found ship, full equipment, and high hopes. We had suffered, starved, and triumphed, groveled down yet grasped at glory, grown bigger in the bigness of the whole. We had seen God in His splendours, heard the text that Nature renders. We had reached the naked soul of man," Shackleton concluded.

CHAPTER 15:

WILL YOU SURVIVE IF YOU RUN AWAY FROM HOME?

What happens to kids who run away from home? Here are but a few stories of their amazing adventures.

For example, have you heard of the 16-year-old runaway who survived more than five hours hidden in the wheel well of an airplane flight from California to Hawaii, despite the lack of oxygen, and temperatures as cold as 80 below zero?

While many runaway kids end up trafficked by others or worse, some brave runaways become famous or at least have a really great story to tell after their escapades.

One American leader every kid learns about in school, Ben Franklin, only came to the city of Philadelphia because he ran away from his family in Boston. He worked as an apprentice in his half-brother James's print shop, but the brothers fought when James refused to publish Franklin's writing.

Ben got a little tricky and started writing well-received letters under the world's greatest pseudonym, "Mrs. Silence Dogood," but when James found out, he was simply furious. So, Ben Franklin ran away and ended up in Philadelphia, where he went on to find the University of Pennsylvania and do some other cool stuff (like discovering electricity, signing the Declaration of Independence, and so on).

In case you didn't know, Harry Houdini was the world-famous master showman who could make himself disappear, and also escape from underwater boxes, chains, and ropes. He pulled off his first disappearing act when he ran away from home at the age of 12. He left his family, who had immigrated to Milwaukee from Hungary, and jumped on a freight car.

Not much is known about the year Houdini spent away from home, but he possibly spent time in Kansas City. He later got together again with his family in New York, helping to support them by working as a necktie cutter and a photographer's assistant. The first job definitely doesn't exist anymore, while the second is pretty rare nowadays. Houdini later became the world's most famous magician and showman.

The real-life teenage trickster played by Leonardo DiCaprio in the movie, Catch Me If You Can, got things rolling as a small-time criminal when he ran away from home at 16. Frank Abagnale Jr. forged checks, pretended he was a doctor, posed as a lawyer, and even claimed to be an airplane pilot to get free flights!

Ultimately, he was caught and served time in French and Swiss prisons before he was turned over to American authorities. Yet he escaped from the airplane used to transport him. After he was captured again, he served five years of his 12-year prison sentence, and then got a job with the FBI, of all people, to help them fight check fraud. He went on to become a security consultant who made millions.

Then there was 17-year-old Barbara McVay who really wanted to go to England in 1966. Her dad was working with the Air Force in the U.K, and as she later told the Sarasota Journal, "I like English boys." One small problem: Barbara lived in Baltimore.

So, she did what any teen probably would do in that case and stowed away on a Britain-bound submarine that happened to be visiting Baltimore. The 1,600-ton submarine (called the Walrus) had been at sea for four hours when Barbara left her hiding place, feeling a little dizzy from carbon monoxide.

Crew members say it's good she left when she did because she'd have drowned when that compartment later filled with water. The Walrus turned around and took Barbara straight back to Baltimore. "We certainly can't have that sort of thing going on in the British Navy," Captain Douglas Scobie stated to the Sarasota Journal: "Taking away one of Baltimore's citizens is rather overextending our appreciation of their hospitality."

In 2007, nine-year-old Semaj Booker really wanted to see his grandfather in Texas. His solution? He decided to steal a car (which he learned how to do from playing some specific video games) and then led police on a high-speed chase.

The police did catch up with him and brought him home. But the very next day he hopped a bus to the airport and managed to snag a plane ticket to Phoenix after using a fake name. The cops picked him up again when he tried to get to Dallas. In 2010, the 13-year-old Booker had another encounter with the police when he supposedly stole a yo-yo from a store.

CHAPTER 16:

PASABAN, THE QUEEN OF 8,000 METERS

As a child, Edurne Pasaban was raised in the Basque region of Spain, which is full of mountains. She climbed her very first mountain when she was 14. In college, she decided to study engineering, but she also didn't want just a nine-to-five job. She simply couldn't keep away from those very, very high mountains for long.

In May of 2010, she completed her biggest challenge ever: climbing the world's 14 tallest mountains. Of course, Edurne became famous for her many climbing achievements, yet she claims she doesn't climb to become renowned. "For me," she emphasizes, "adventure is a way of life."

Edurne Pasaban became the first woman to climb all 14 mountains over 8,000 meters (26,246 feet) in May 2010. Those peaks span the nations of Nepal, China, India, and Pakistan. They range from Shisha Pangma in Tibet at 26,335 feet to the biggest of the big, Everest in Nepal, which rises to 29,029 feet. Standing on the summit of a majestic mountain, the Spanish mountaineer is at her happiest. "I feel free, without any pressure of any kind. I am at peace with myself," she reports.

At almost the same time, South Korean climber Oh Eun-Sun appeared to beat Pasaban in their race to be the first to complete the 14 massive mountain peaks. It seemed that back in 2010, Oh managed to scale all 14 some three weeks before Pasaban did the same daunting feat.

However, fellow climbers began to question whether Oh had reached the summit of Kanchenjunga, one of the mountains on that mighty list, the previous year. After a complete investigation by the Korean Alpine Federation in August 2010, they concluded that Oh had not completed the ascent. Thus, Pasaban was generally considered to be the first female to scale all 14 peaks.

On the other hand, Oh spoke out about her own grand achievement. The Asian climber replied to the question on a KBS (Korean) talk show on whether she had really scaled the peak: "The god of Kanchenjunga knows that. And I've never deceived the god."

Whether the god of that mountain had really witnessed Oh at its soaring summit, the real problem was that the climber herself couldn't provide a convincing photo of herself at the top - for various reasons.

While this final adventurous chapter is mainly about Pasaban, it's interesting to look at her Korean rival who certainly had her fair share of adventures on some of our globe's loftiest peaks, where the oxygen is so thin that you would struggle to take a step or two.

Oh Eun-Sun's father served in the South Korean military, and the family moved a lot during her early childhood, eventually settling in Seoul. During high school, she took up rock climbing as an adventure-filled hobby. In 1985, she entered the University of Suwon, where she decided to major in computer science and naturally became a member of the mountaineering club.

After graduating, she became a civil servant in Seoul, a job she left in the early 1990s to join a group composed only of women planning an expedition up Mount Everest. After a period of rigorous training in 1993, she climbed Everest to 23,950 feet with the team, but she was unable to reach the summit on that occasion.

Disappointed at her failure to make it to the top, Oh resolved to train even harder. She reached the summit of her first 26,246 feet peak in 1997 when she scaled Gasherbrum II (26,361 feet) in the Karakoram Range (which lies on the border between Pakistani and Chinese-administered portions of the Kashmir Region).

In 1999, she went on to attempt two more summits—Broad Peak (26,401 feet), also in the Karakorum's, and Makalu (27,766 feet), which rises in the Himalayas located between Nepal and China (actually Tibet), but she couldn't reach the top of either one on those occasions either.

After Oh's failure in 2001 to make it to the mighty summit of what's called K2 (located in the Karakorum's and rising to 28,251 feet high), the world's second highest peak, she stopped attempting 26,246-feet mountains for a period to concentrate on some other of the world's noteworthy peaks.

Between 2002 and 2004, she climbed the highest points on each of the seven continents, including Mount Everest in 2004, a feat she accomplished "solo" (in fact, nobody climbs the world's highest mountains alone, but there are clearly different levels of support). She added Jaya Peak in Indonesia, the highest mountain to be found on an island, to her list of achievements in 2006.

After her successful ascent of Everest, she continued her conquest of the world's 26,246-foot peaks. She scaled one called Xixabangma (which sits to the northwest of Everest and measures 26,286 feet) in 2006, two in 2007 (including K2), and four each in 2008 (including Broad Peak and Makalu) and 2009.

That set the stage for her climb of the final mountain in the group, Annapurna I (26,545 feet) in Nepal. She wasn't successful on her first attempt in 2009, turning back just short of the summit because of bad weather (imagine climbing your socks off to almost 26,246 feet, and then having the weather turn against you!).

However, she did top the mountain on April 27, 2010, even finishing the incredible climb on her hands and knees. Then came the controversy about whether Oh or Pasaban was actually the first woman to complete the world's 14 rock masses that reach 26,246 feet.

If somebody goes that high, that often, and claims to be the first to do so, they need proof. The controversy was partly caused by a photo of Oh that was supposed to have been taken at the summit - a claim Pasaban disputed. Another problem was the conflicting testimony of the Sherpa guides who accompanied her up that mountain (one guide said she made it, while another said she didn't).

Both sides agreed to accept the judgment of Elizabeth Hawley, an individual who's long been regarded as mountaineering's unofficial record keeper and historian. When Hawley interviewed Oh after her return from climbing Annapurna, Hawley accepted Oh's version of the events on Kanchenjunga, while at the same time listing the ascent as "disputed."

However, in June 2010, Hawley changed her story, saying then it was "unlikely" that Oh had reached the top of the mountain. Two months later, the Alpine Korean Federation stated that she'd "probably failed" to reach the rarified summit of Kanchenjunga. Nevertheless, Oh no doubt had some amazing adventures, and many close calls, while she hiked and climbed in the thinnest air on this planet Earth.

But let's get back to Pasaban: When she was born in the Basque region of Spain, she suffered from a stomach illness that wasn't diagnosed until she was already six. "I had few ambitions when I was a child," she explains. "I had a lot of fears and very low self-esteem. I hardly communicated with other children my age."

As a kid, Pasaban enjoyed trekking with her parents in Basque Country. At the age of 14, she first joined a mountaineering club and got into climbing, initially in the Pyrenees and the Alps, before progressing to the higher Himalayas.

It took Pasaban nine years, from 2001 to 2010, to climb all those mountains. When she climbed Manaslu in 2008, Pasaban claims that it snowed for most of the ascent, not only making it hard to see but creating extremely dangerous slippery conditions for even the most experienced climber.

"After climbing Everest, I realized this was my passion, and that the path I wanted to follow was to do expeditions," Pasaban claims. "My father made me face the dilemma of choosing between my engineering career and concentrating on professional climbing. At that moment, I heard my heart."

Pasaban didn't set out to make history. She'd already climbed nine of the 14 biggest mountains, including this ascent of 27,939-feet Lhotse in 2003, when it became clear to her that she could complete them all.

"I started climbing the 8,000-ers because I really enjoyed it, and also maybe out of love," she elaborates. "I never considered the possibility of finishing them until the end. That possibility arose when I had climbed nine mountains."

In 2011, Pasaban attempted to climb Everest for a second time. She decided to pass on the artificial oxygen, but then couldn't reach the summit without it. "This is an outstanding challenge," she affirms. "I would not like to finish my career without having achieved it, but I have to find the right moment in my professional life to do it. It is a dream."

If climbing the world's tallest mountains isn't enough, Pasaban is now working away as an executive coach and lecturer, and she runs her own travel agency as well. In addition, she plans to climb more 6,000- and 7,000-meter (19,685- and 22,965-feet) mountains, especially in that magical mountain kingdom known as Tibet.

If you don't succeed the first time, try again. In some cases, you may need to try five times. Pasaban finally reached the summit of Shisha Pangma on her fifth attempt in 2010, which was the last of her 14 mountains.

Mountaineering is clearly a risky sport, and Pasaban said she has lost 15 dear friends in all her years of climbing. One member of her own team perished on her ascent of Dhaulagiri in the Himalayas in 2001.

Pasaban speaks candidly about fighting off depression which she believed was triggered in part by what she had to sacrifice: her career and the possibility of having children. "It was a critical moment in my life, and I nearly wanted to give up all," she explains.

"Trying to find the incentive to continue a lot of times is not easy, and when you're suffering from depression, it's even harder, because you don't see beyond yourself. For me, the fourteen 8,000-ers have been more than 14 mountains - they've been the key to come out from where I was," Edurne admitted.

Pasaban was asked how climbing very tall mountains had changed her. "I could admire the splendor of the Himalayas. After having climbed all over the world, being at the foot of an 8,000-meter mountain made me realize how small we are compared to nature, which made me respect it.

"After that first time, I've been back to the Himalayas many times, and I learned a lot after that experience. I learned to value my life more. Seeing beautiful landscapes made me understand how lucky we are to see such amazing places with our own eyes, and I dream about having a long life to be able to see more beautiful places," Pasaban stated.

What was it that surprised Pasaban the most while she was making her way up so many magnificent mountains? "The hospitality of the people in Nepal surprised me. They don't have a lot, but they share all they have with you. They care about you, and above all, their smiles. We live in a society in which we don't receive or see a smile very often. In places like Nepal, they smile at you all the time," she recalled with a wide grin.

You might guess that since she studied engineering, Pasaban gets into planning her ascents a bit more than some others. "I like planning things, although I sometimes should be more flexible. As an engineer, I'm definitely a planner, and I've realized that I apply this to my trips and life. But I'm easy to adapt to changes," Pasaban emphasized.

CONCLUSION

As an adventurous kid, what kind of amazing adventure story do you like most? We assume that you found every kind of incredible adventure story here that you could ever possibly ask for - from a teenage girl falling from a doomed plane two miles through thin air into a dense jungle, and living to tell the tale, to kids who run away from home (or are forced to leave their homes), to youngsters the same age as you who survive sudden avalanches, ferocious fires, and falling into prickly bushes (which save them from falling off a much bigger cliff!).

Once upon a time, a popular singer sang: "I will survive!" Although she was clearly expressing herself in a more figurative sense (about "surviving" a romantic breakup), her song seems especially appropriate for all of these amazing survival stories.

So, if you ever come face to face with a sharp-toothed alligator by surprise, and it hasn't had its lunch yet, keep repeating: "I will survive!" And then, go for it! But for now, we hope you simply enjoy these amazing survival stories for adventurous kids - from the cozy comfort of your couch.

Made in the USA
Middletown, DE
06 March 2024

50917213R00080